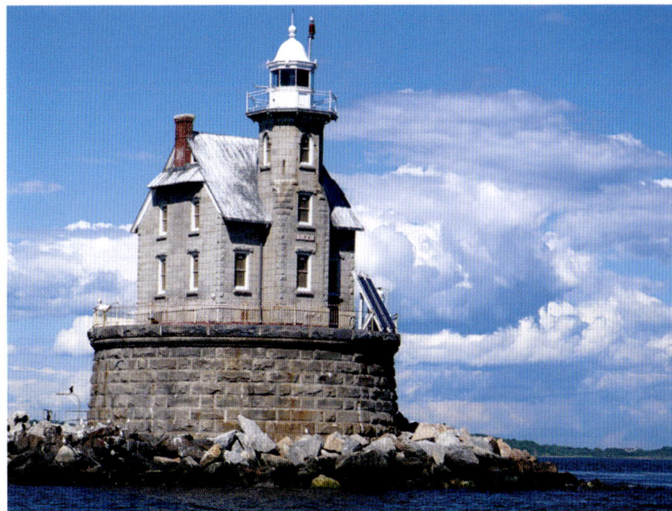

NEW YORK STATE

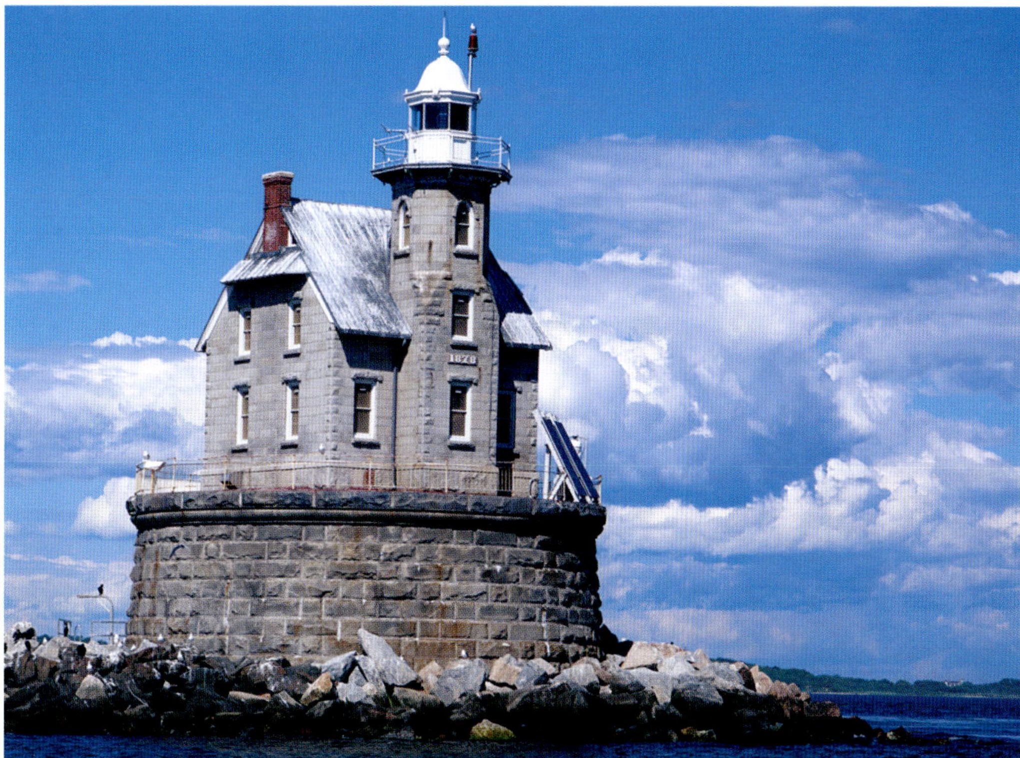

AMERICA SERIES

Text by Helen Stortini
Edited by Ben D'Andrea
Photo editing by Helen Stortini
Cover and interior design by Steve Penner
Typeset by Helen Stortini

Printed and bound in China

Library and Archives Canada Cataloguing in Publication
Stortini, Helen
New York State / Helen Stortini.
(America series)
ISBN 978-1-94041-619-9
1. New York (State)—Pictorial works. I. Cohen, David, 1955-II. Title. III. Series.
F120.S76 2006 974.7'044'0222 C2006-900326-2

For more information on the America Series titles, please visit Midpoint Trade Books at www.midpointtrade.com.

Fog shrouds the valleys of the rolling Adirondack Mountains. Brilliant red and gold leaves sway in the Catskills' gentle autumn breeze. Mist rises from the thunderous sheer drop of Niagara Falls. Endless rows of grapevines converge towards the sandy shores of the narrow Finger Lakes. Manhattan city streets buzz with their eternal hustle and bustle. These are just a few of the diverse pleasures that New York State has to offer.

But there's more to the state than the glamor of big cities and the serenity of the countryside. New York played a key role in the birth of a nation. During the American Revolution, the state witnessed many crucial battles, including the decisive one at Saratoga. This American defeat of British troops initiated the French-American alliance, which ultimately helped secure an American victory. Already at that time one of the world's most exciting cities, New York City was declared the new nation's first capital. It was here that George Washington was inaugurated as the first president.

In 1825, the opening of the Erie Canal further extended the importance of "The Empire State." Access to the Great Lakes turned New York into a vital port and industrial center. As a result of the new economic activity the canal generated, the city began to welcome immigrants from around the world, a pattern that continues to this day.

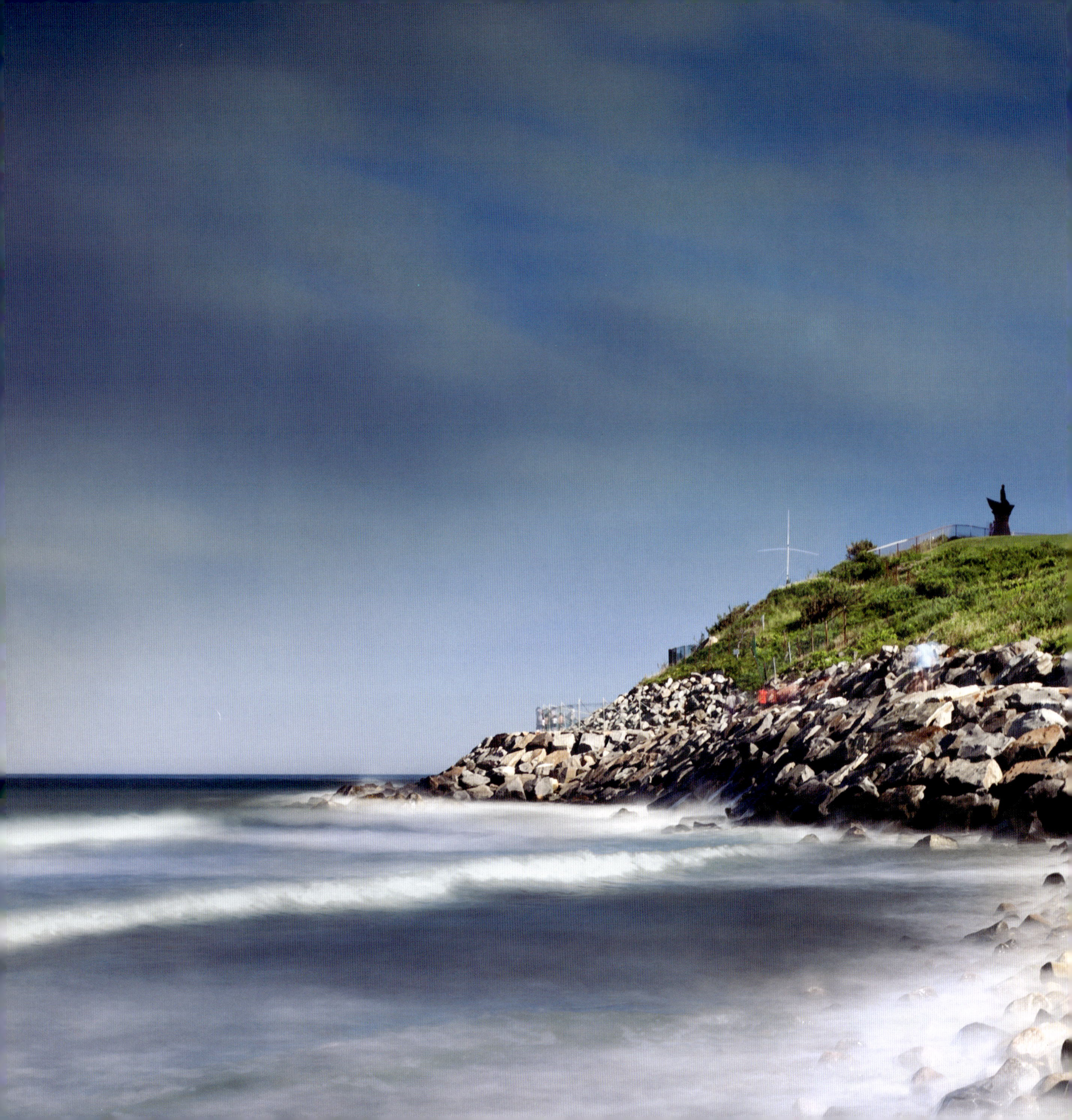

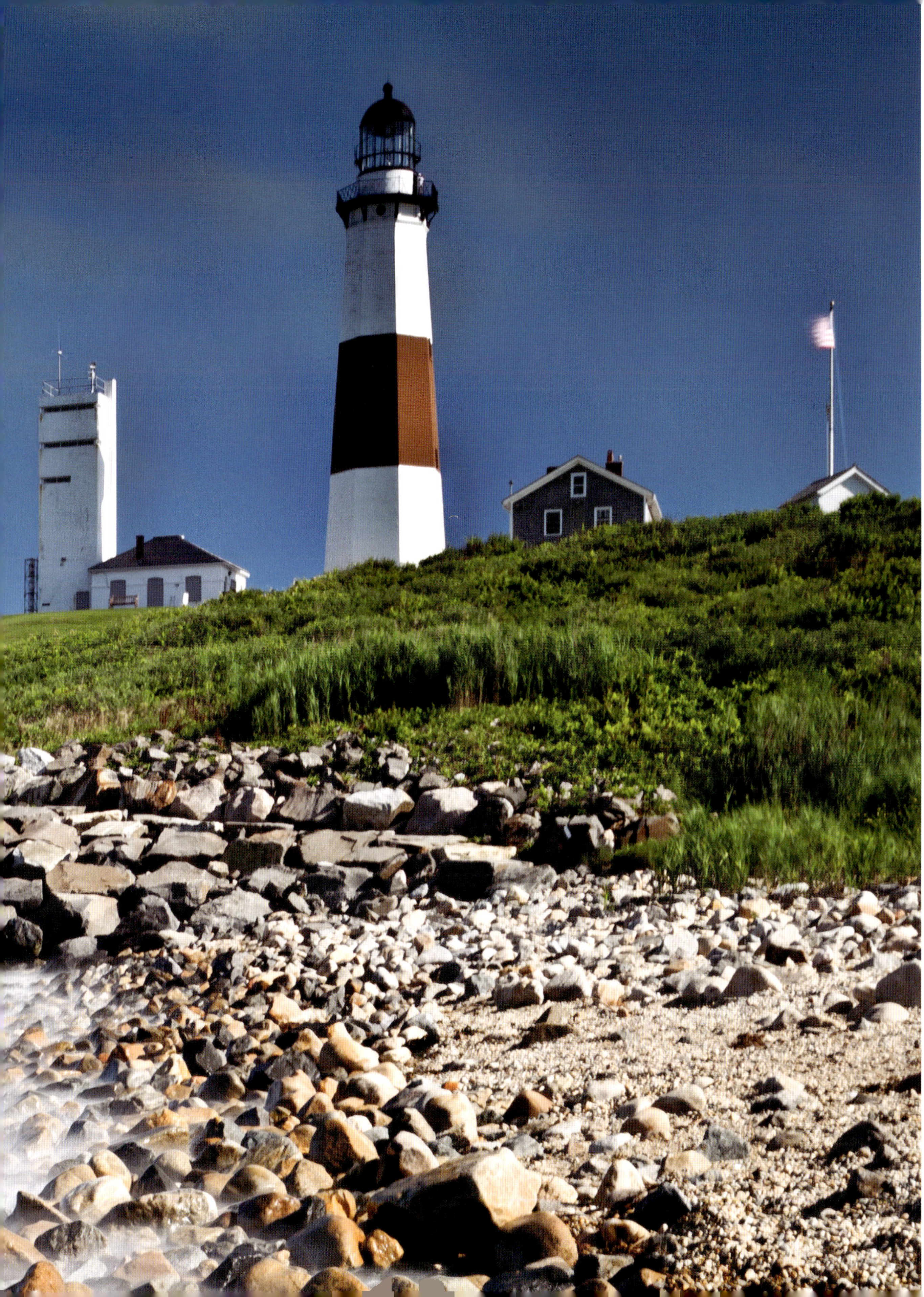

The journey through New York begins with its first lighthouse, Montauk Point, at the easternmost tip of Long Island.

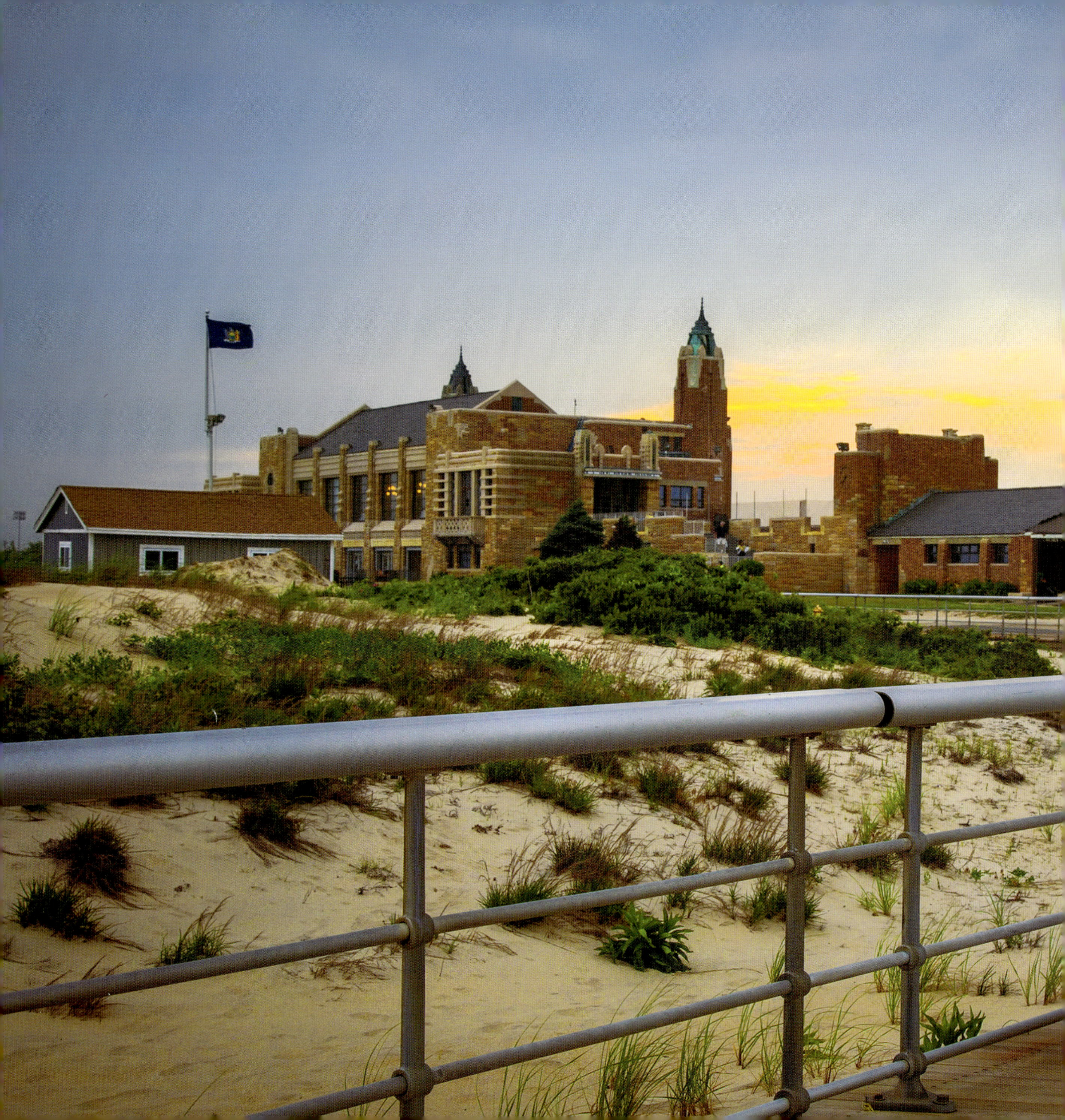

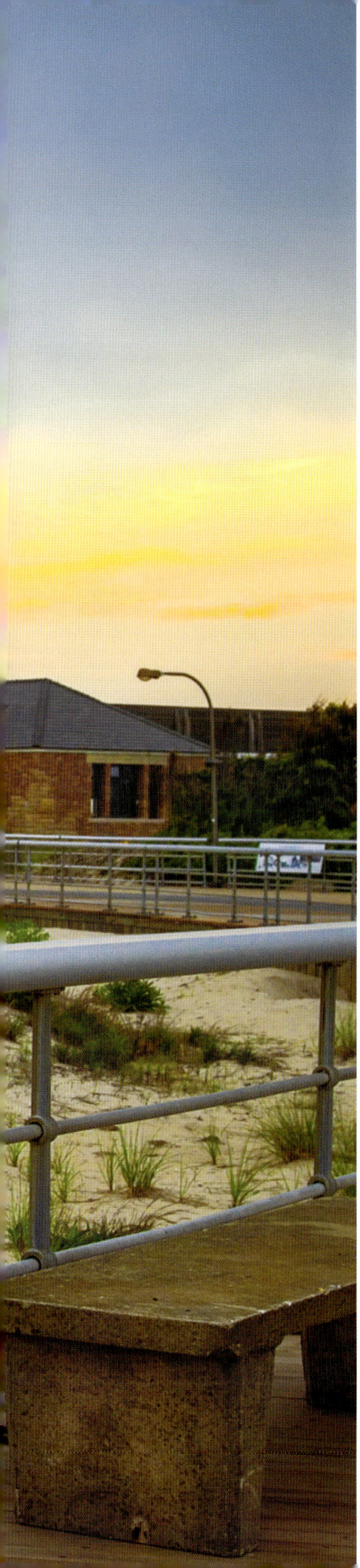

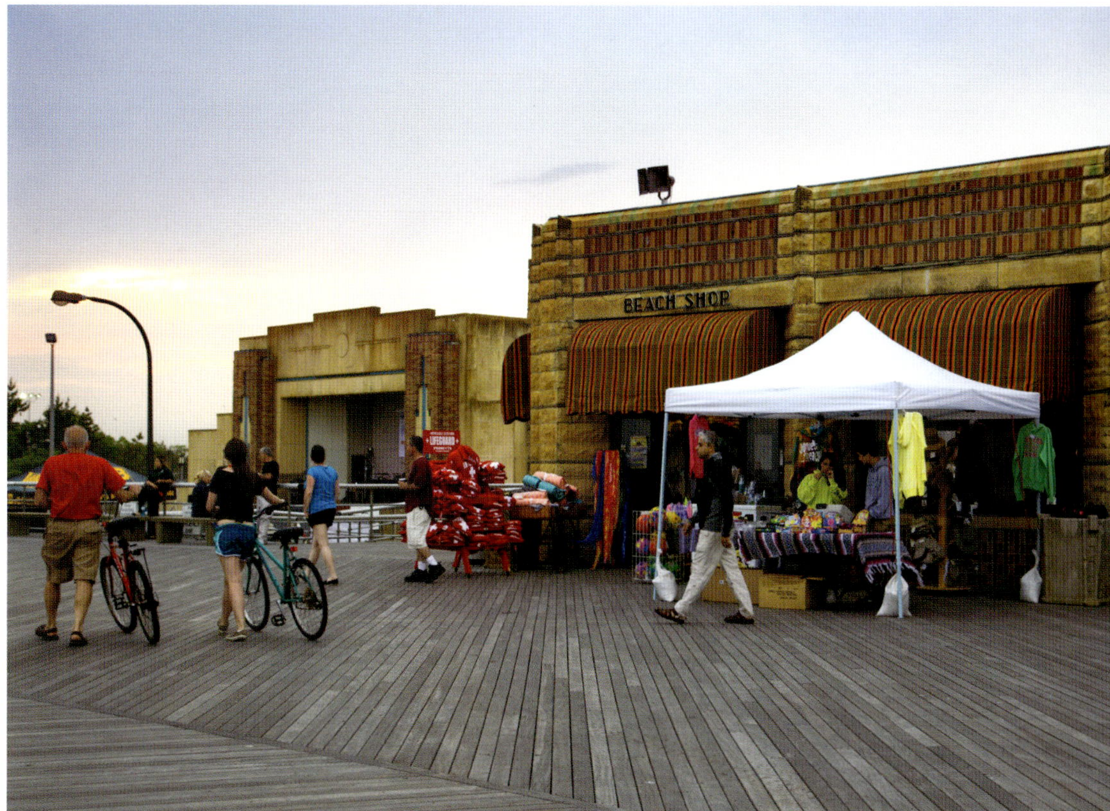

Commissioned by urban planner Robert Moses and opened to the public in 1929, Jones Beach holds boardwalks, beach shops, and bathhouses.

Along the south shore of Long Island is Jones Beach, an over 2,400 acre large playground for suburbanites.

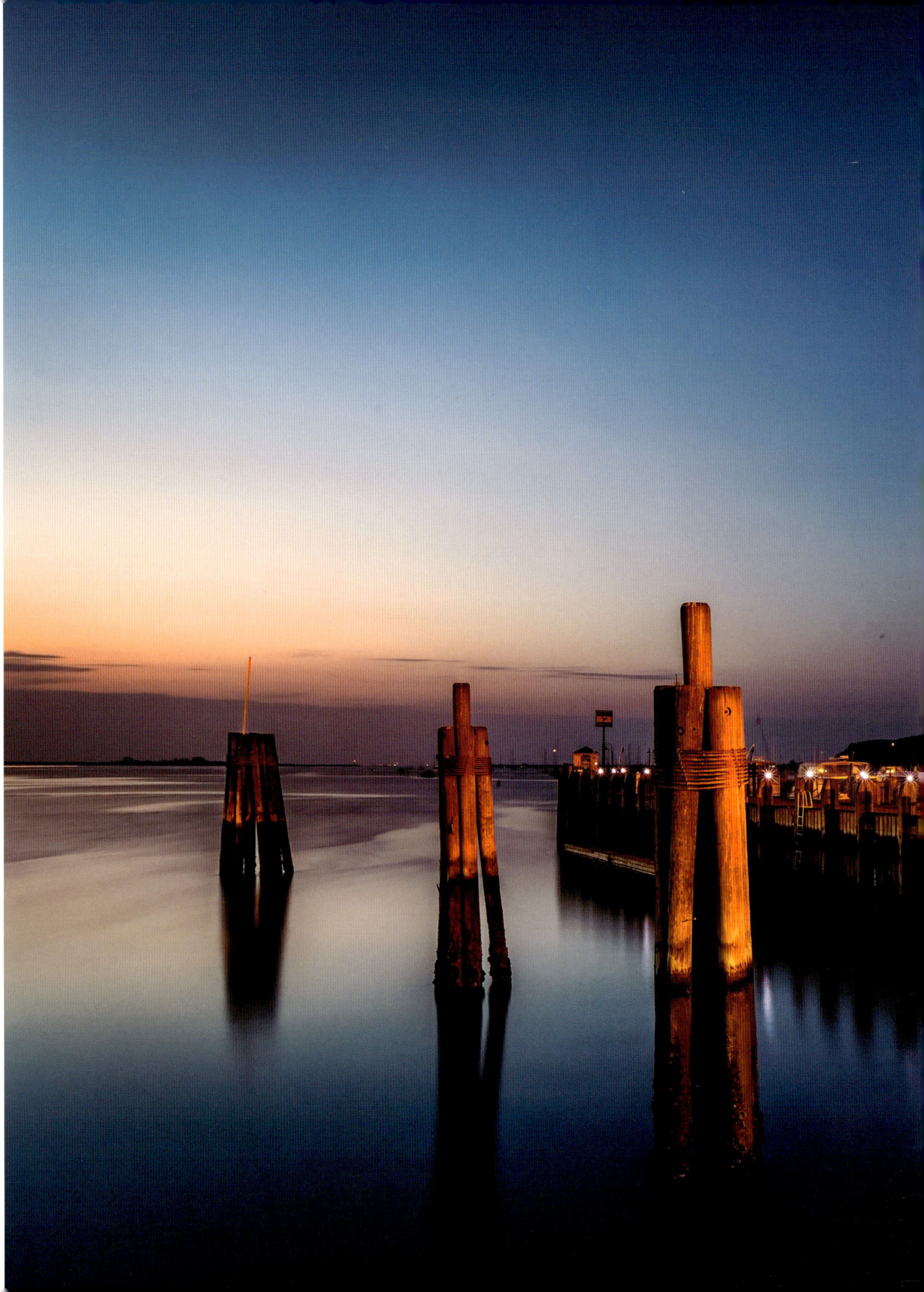

In Port Jefferson, a harbor pier looks over deep waters at dusk. This north shore village maintains a tourist-based economy with its ferries, festivals, restaurants, and shops.

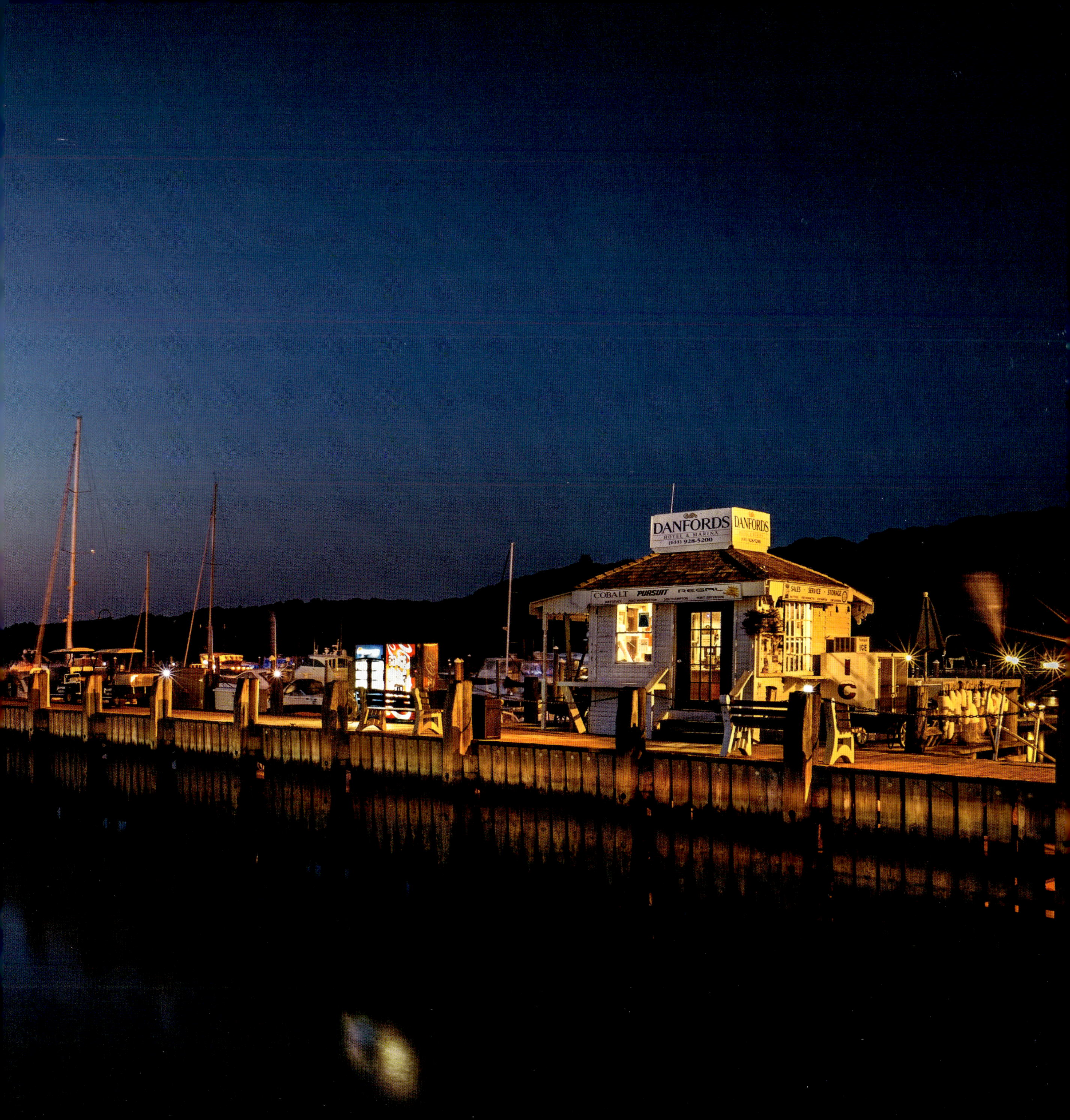
DANFORDS
HOTEL & MARINA
(631) 928-5200
DANFORDS
COBALT PURSUIT REGAL
SOUTHAMPTON
SALES · SERVICE · STORAGE
ICE

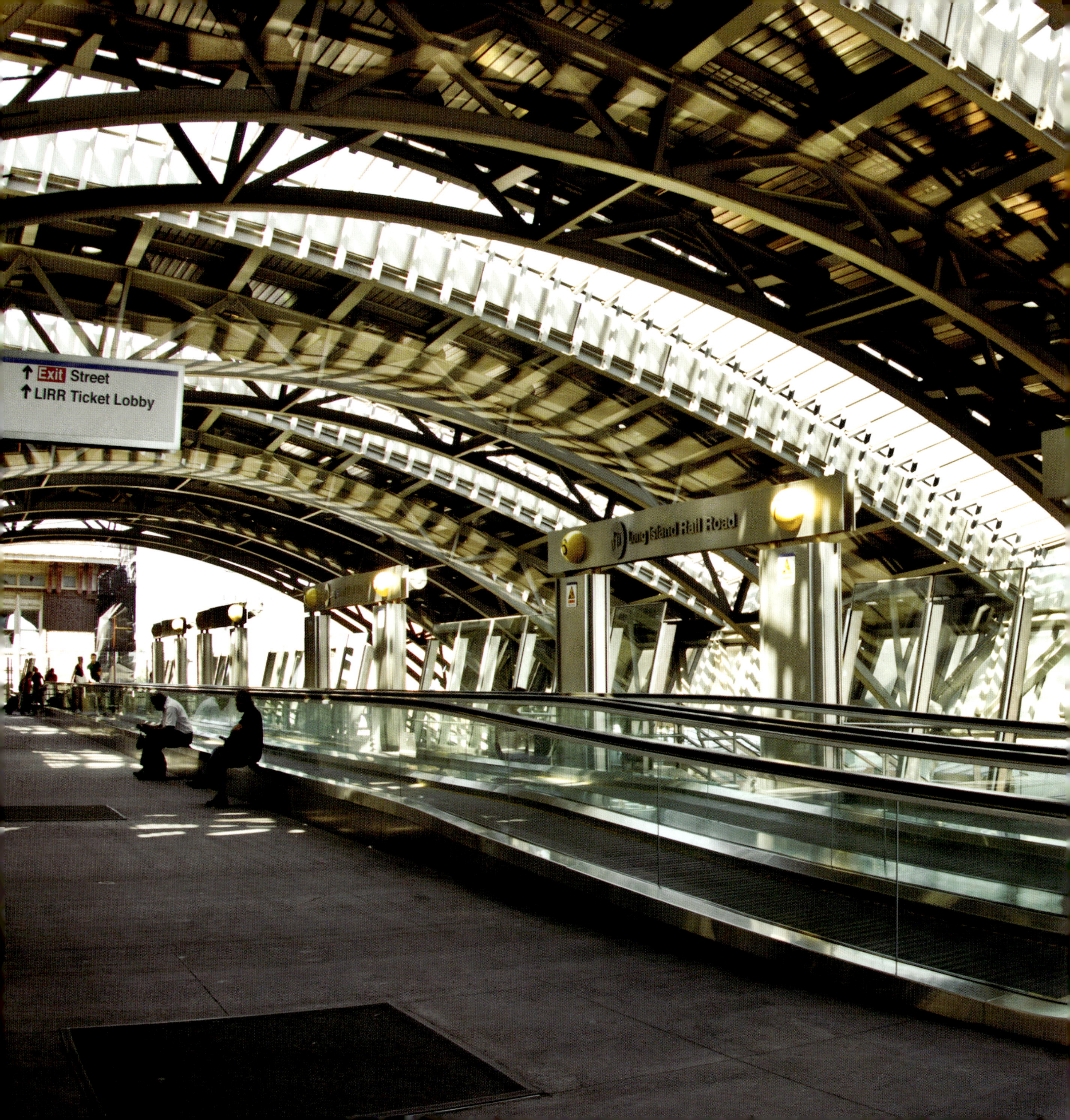
Exit Street
LIRR Ticket Lobby
Long Island Rail Road

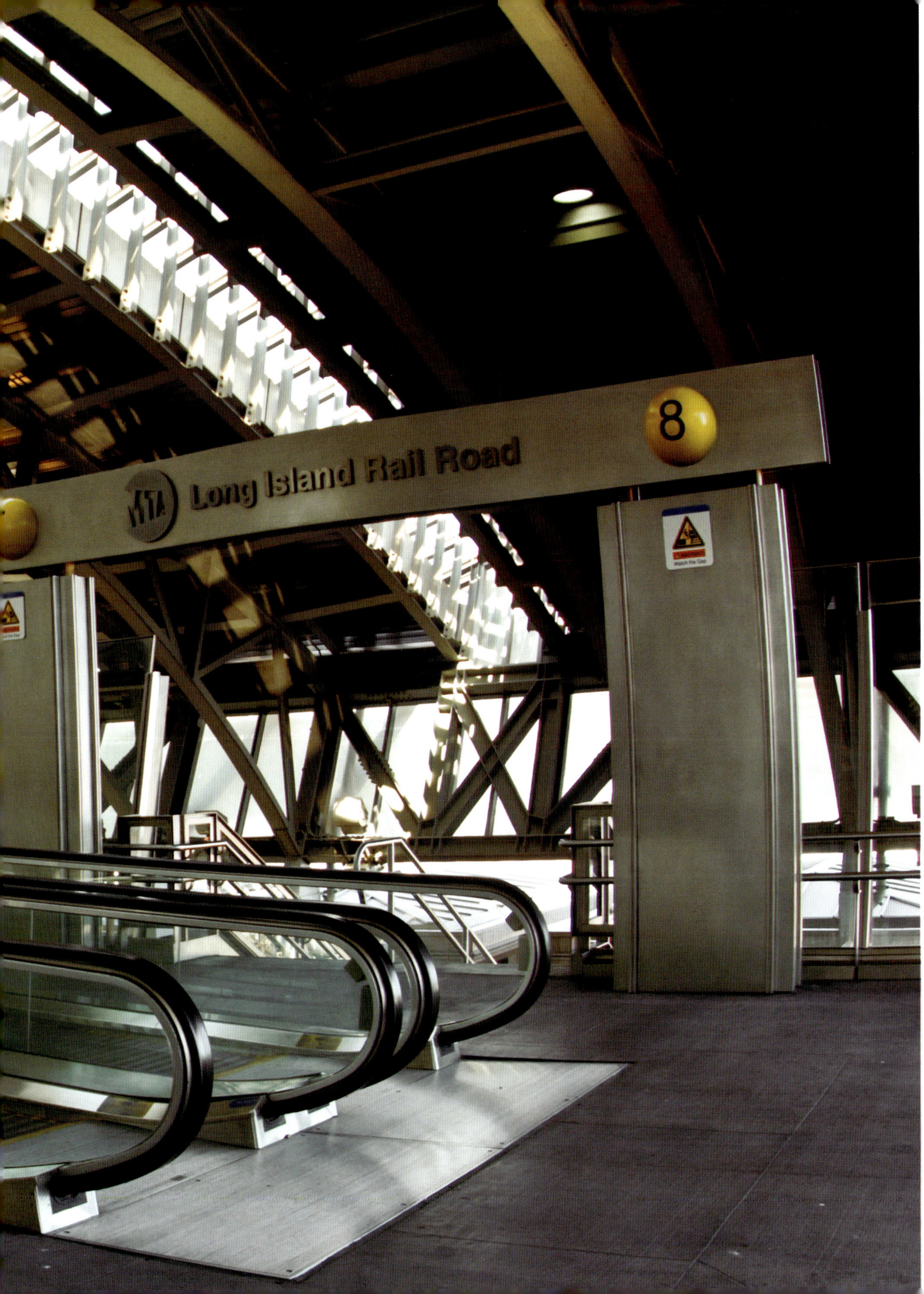

Connecting the island to its metropolitan center is the Long Island Railroad. Every Day, over 200,000 passengers pass through the commuting hub of LIRR's station in Jamaica, Queens.

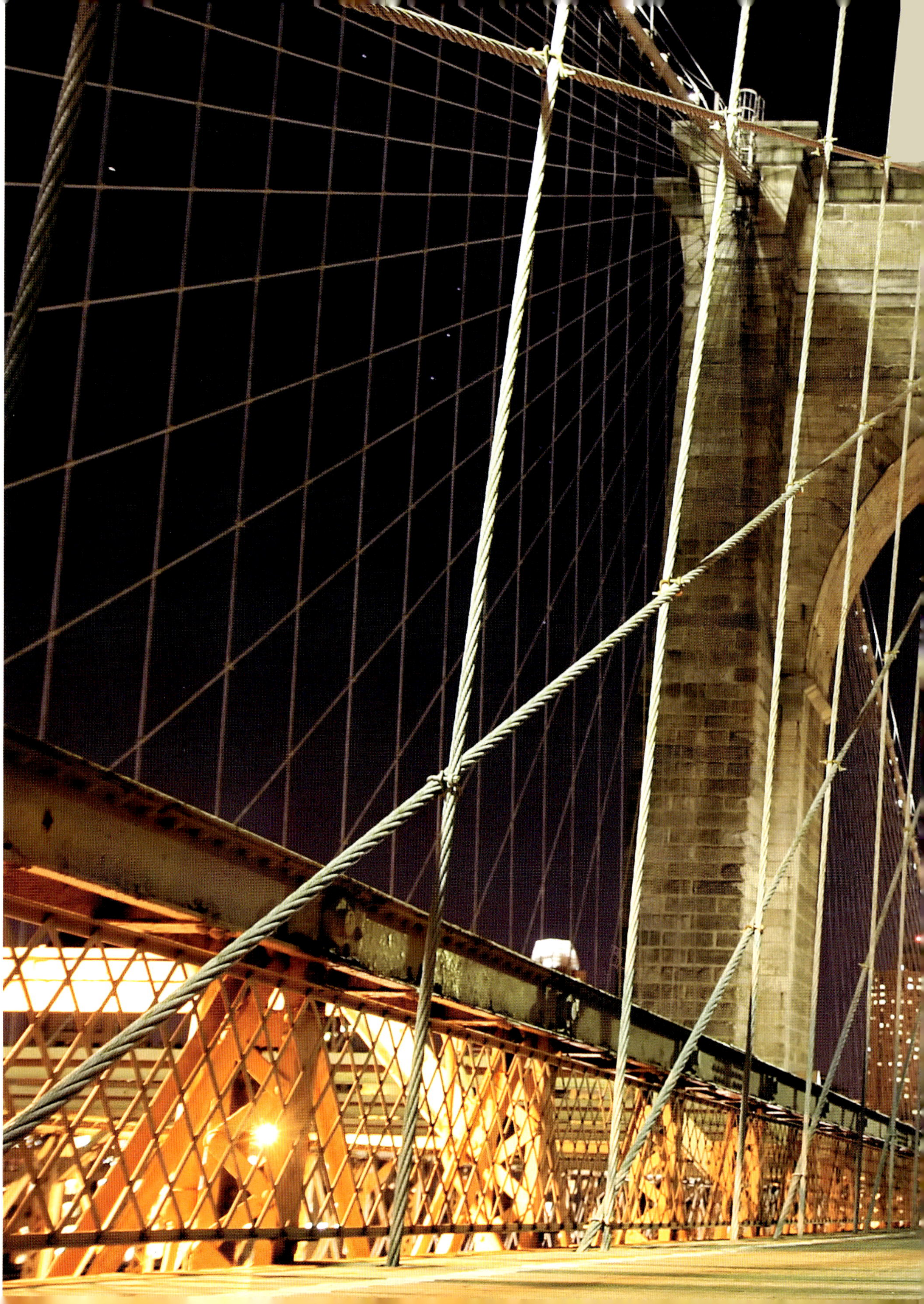

Seen from the pedestrian walkway among bright lights at night, the impressive masonry and steel cables give Brooklyn Bridge its iconic shape.

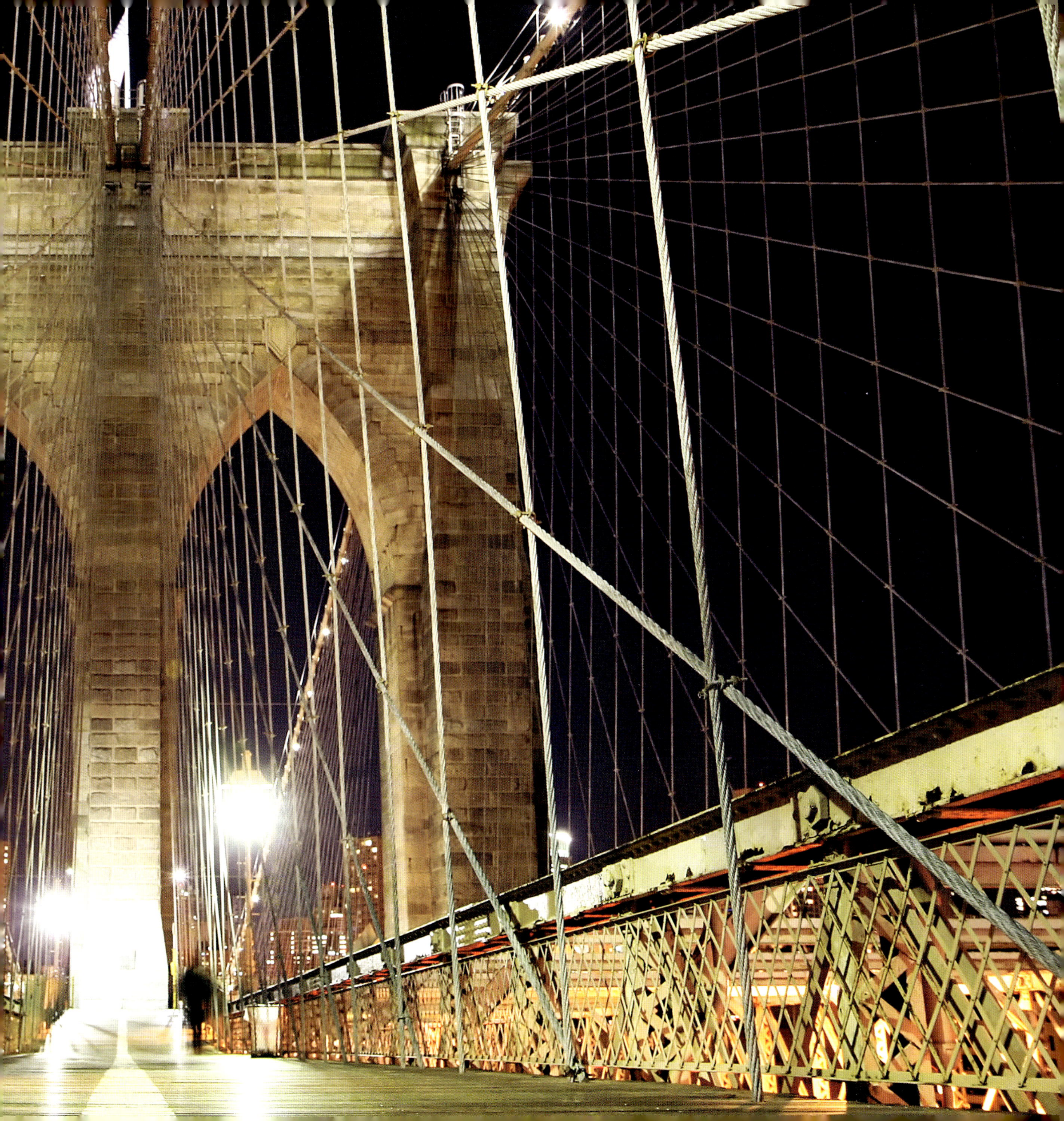

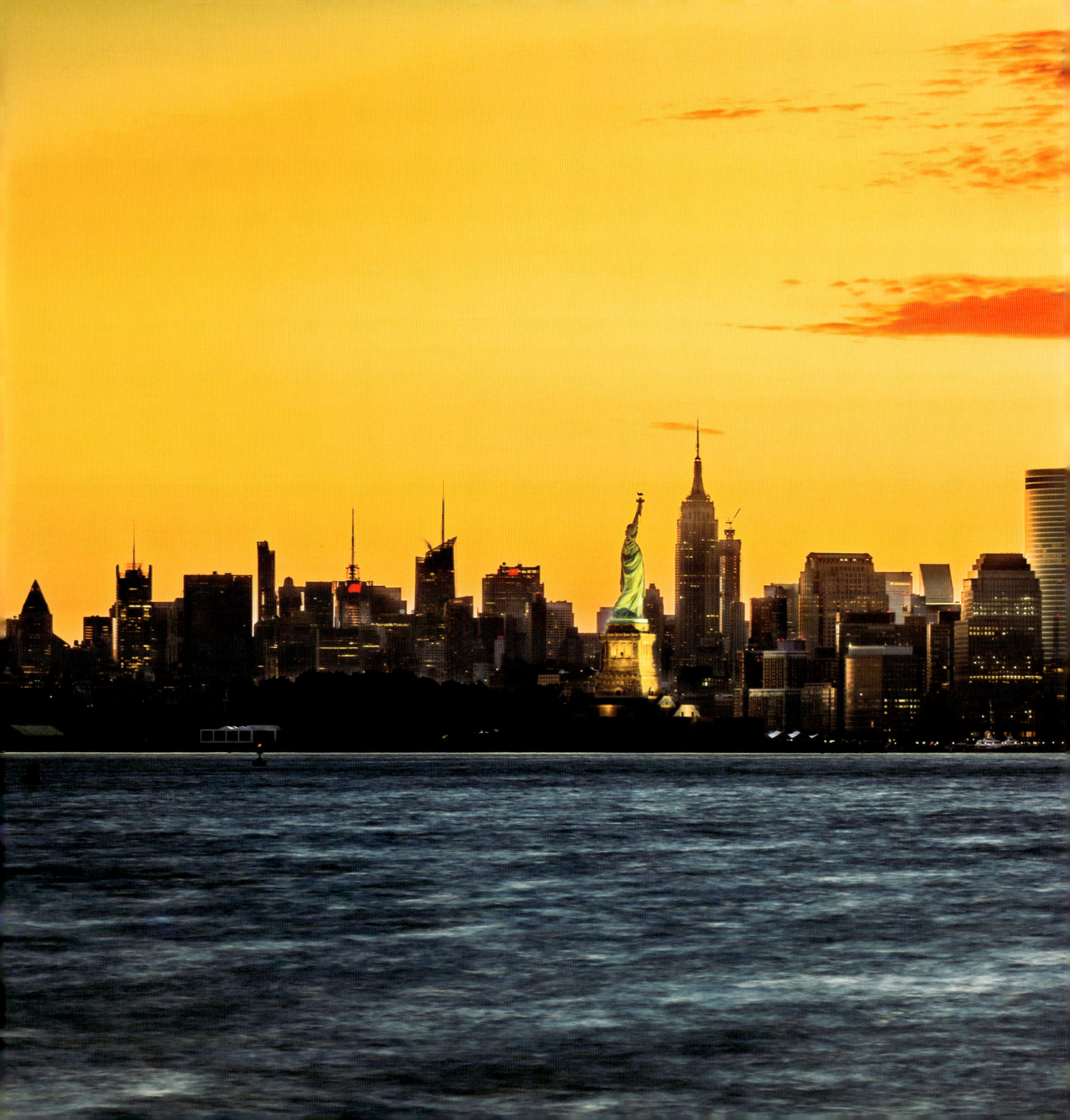

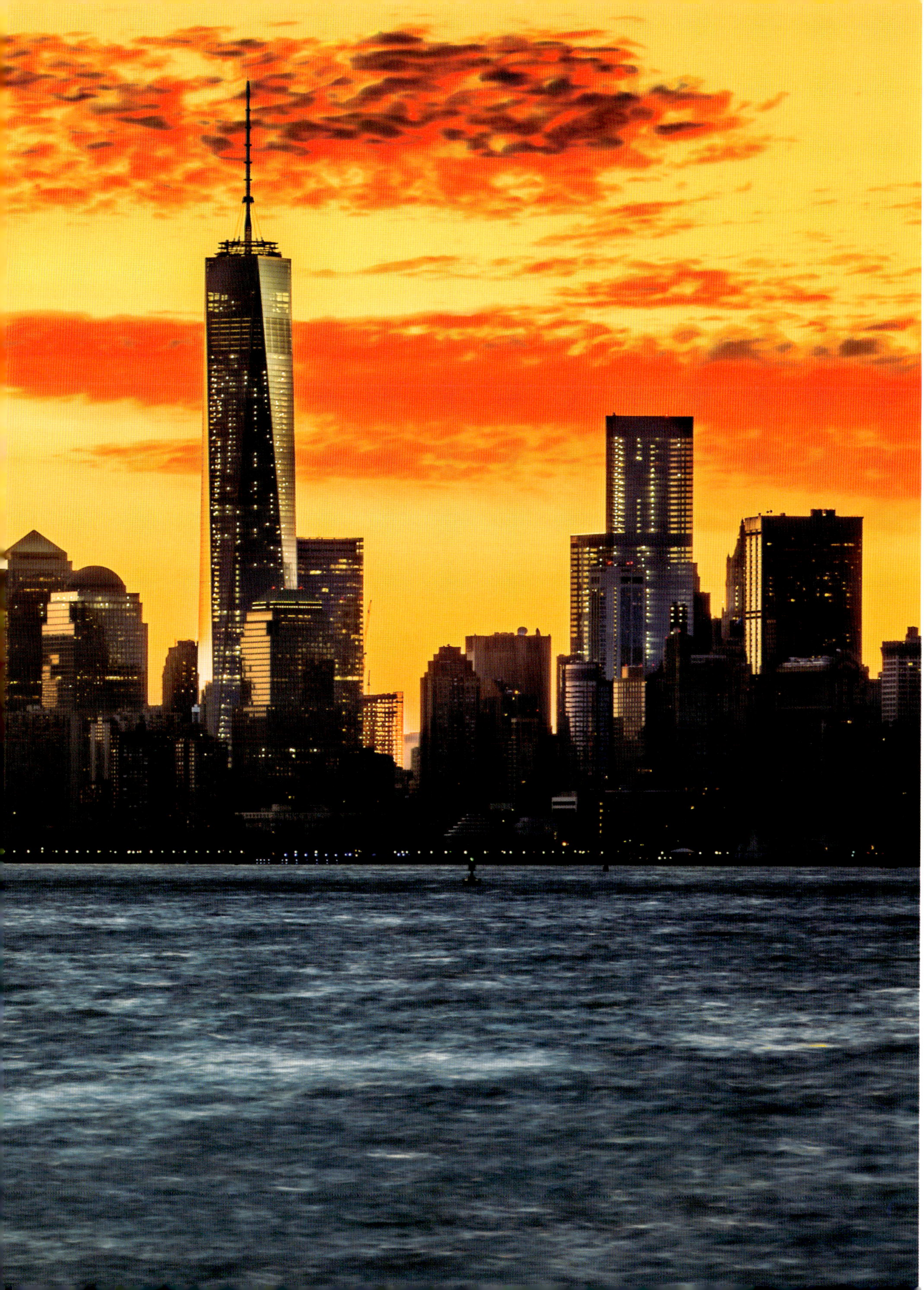

The Freedom Tower rises above the skyline of New York City. More than an international hub for finance, politics, and entertainment, NYC is a densely populated city that over 8 million people call home.

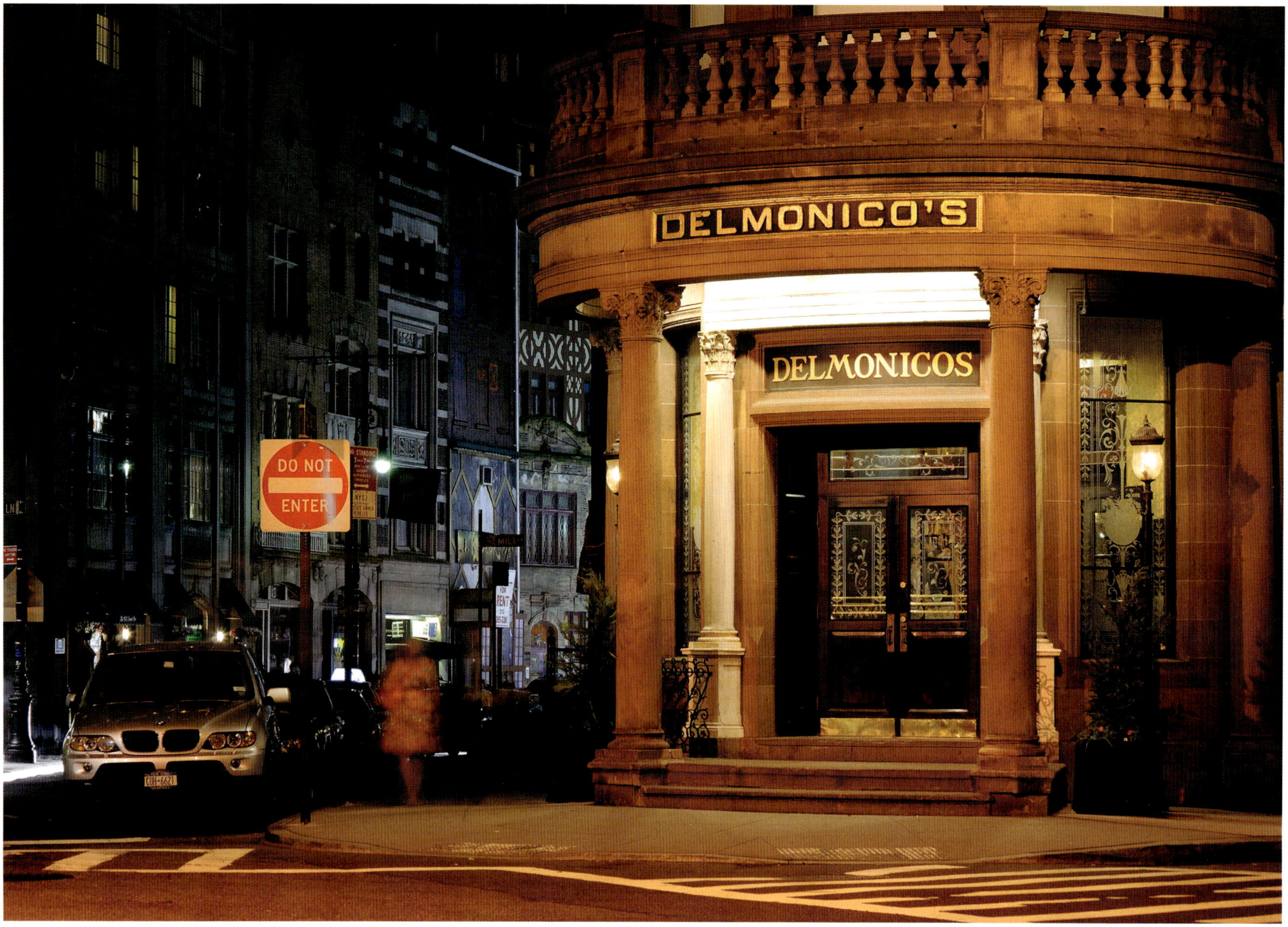

Carrying on in the tradition of its predecessors, the Delmonico's eatery at 56 Beaver Street in the Financial District is known for its signature steaks, Lobster Newburg, and Baked Alaska.

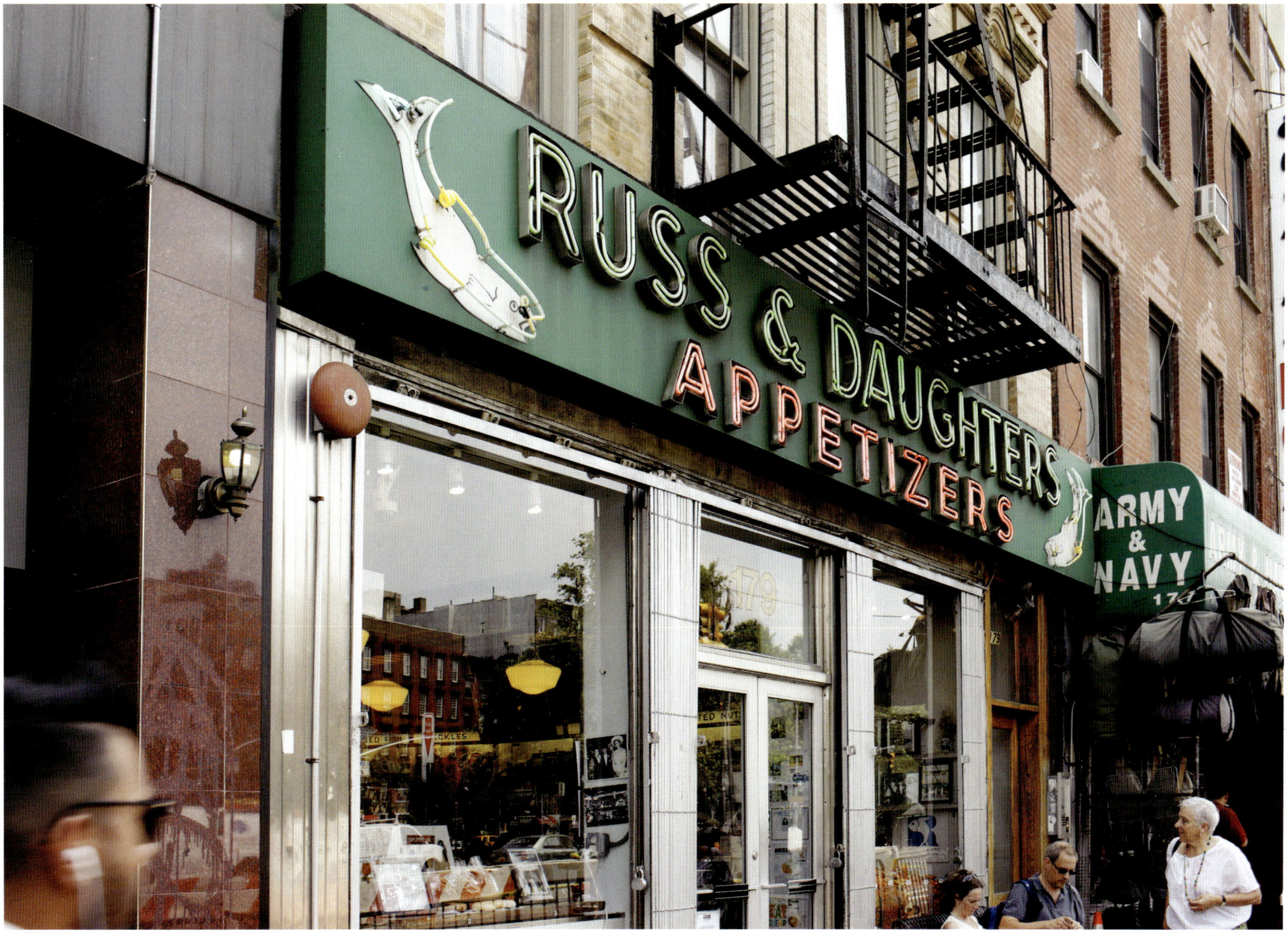

Noted chef and author Anthony Bourdain says the Lower East Side's famous appetizing shop Russ & Daughters "occupies that rare and tiny place on the mountaintop reserved for those who are not just the oldest and the last—but also the best."

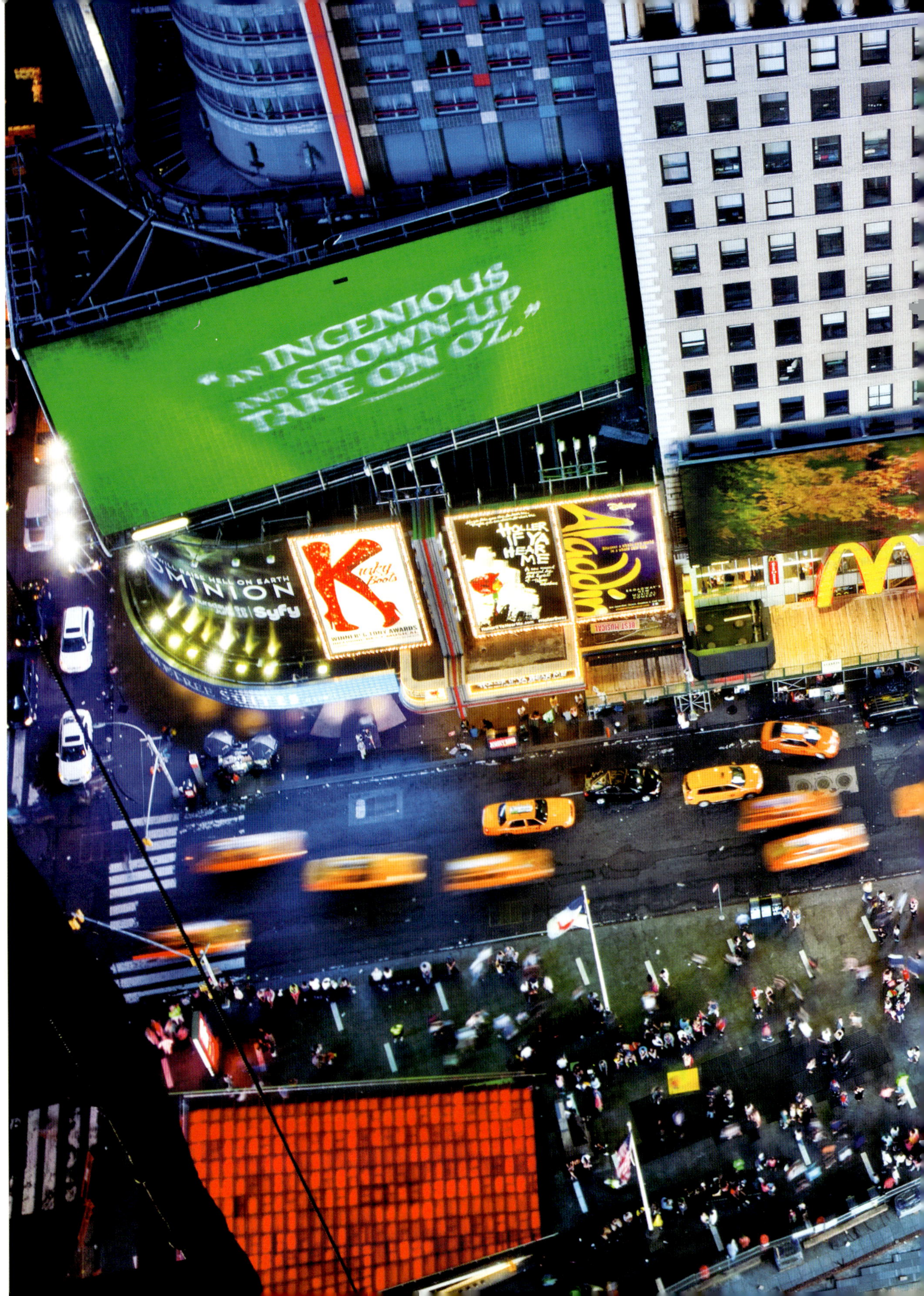

A dizzying aerial view captures the bright lights and billboards of Times Square, named for the one-time headquarters of the New York Times. A hub for Broadway theaters and a popular destination for New Year's Eve, the area is constantly abuzz.

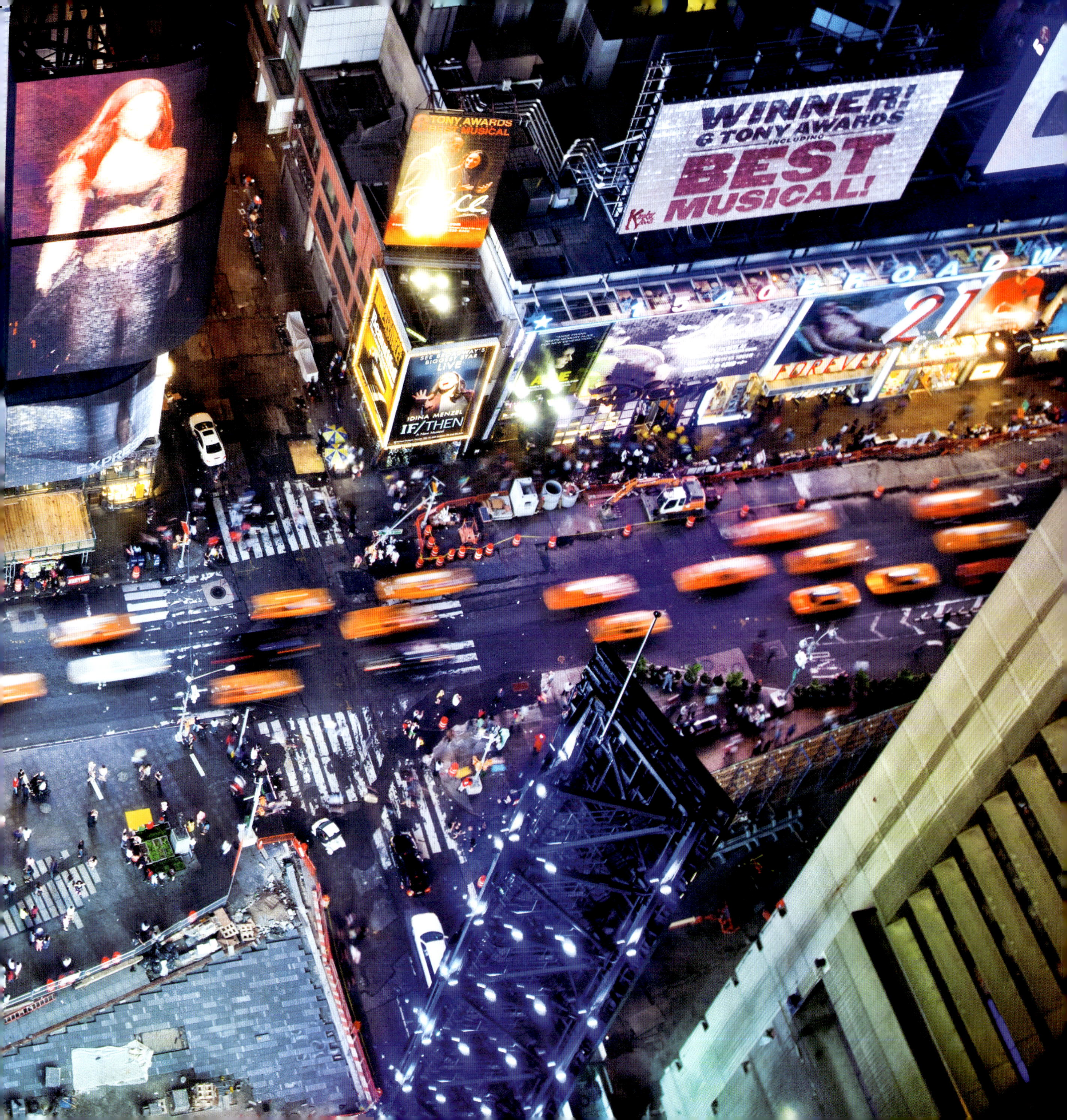
WINNER!
6 TONY AWARDS
INCLUDING
BEST
MUSICAL!
1540 BROADWAY
FOREVER 21
IDINA MENZEL
IF/THEN
TONY AWARDS
BEST MUSICAL

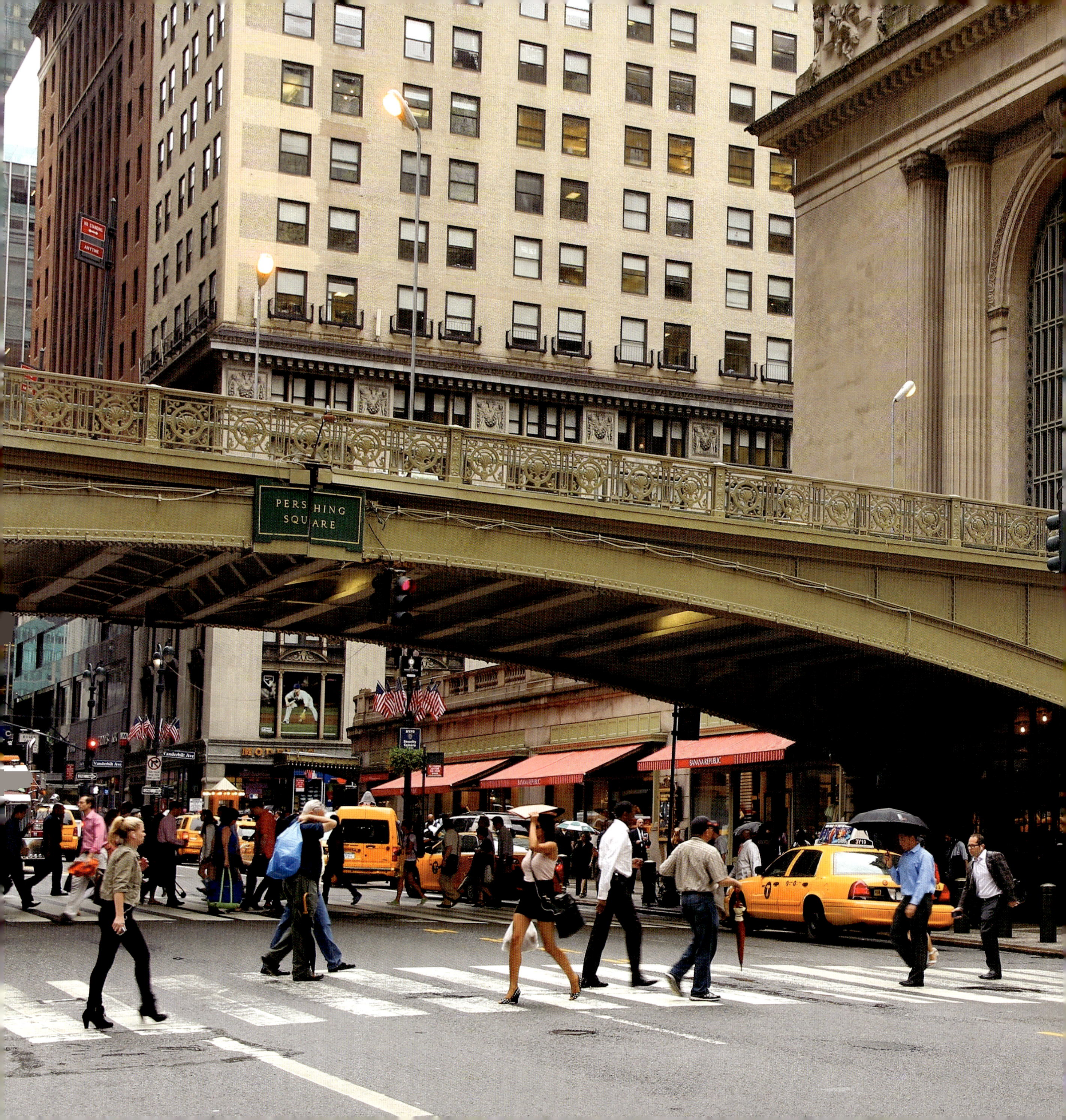
PERSHING
SQUARE

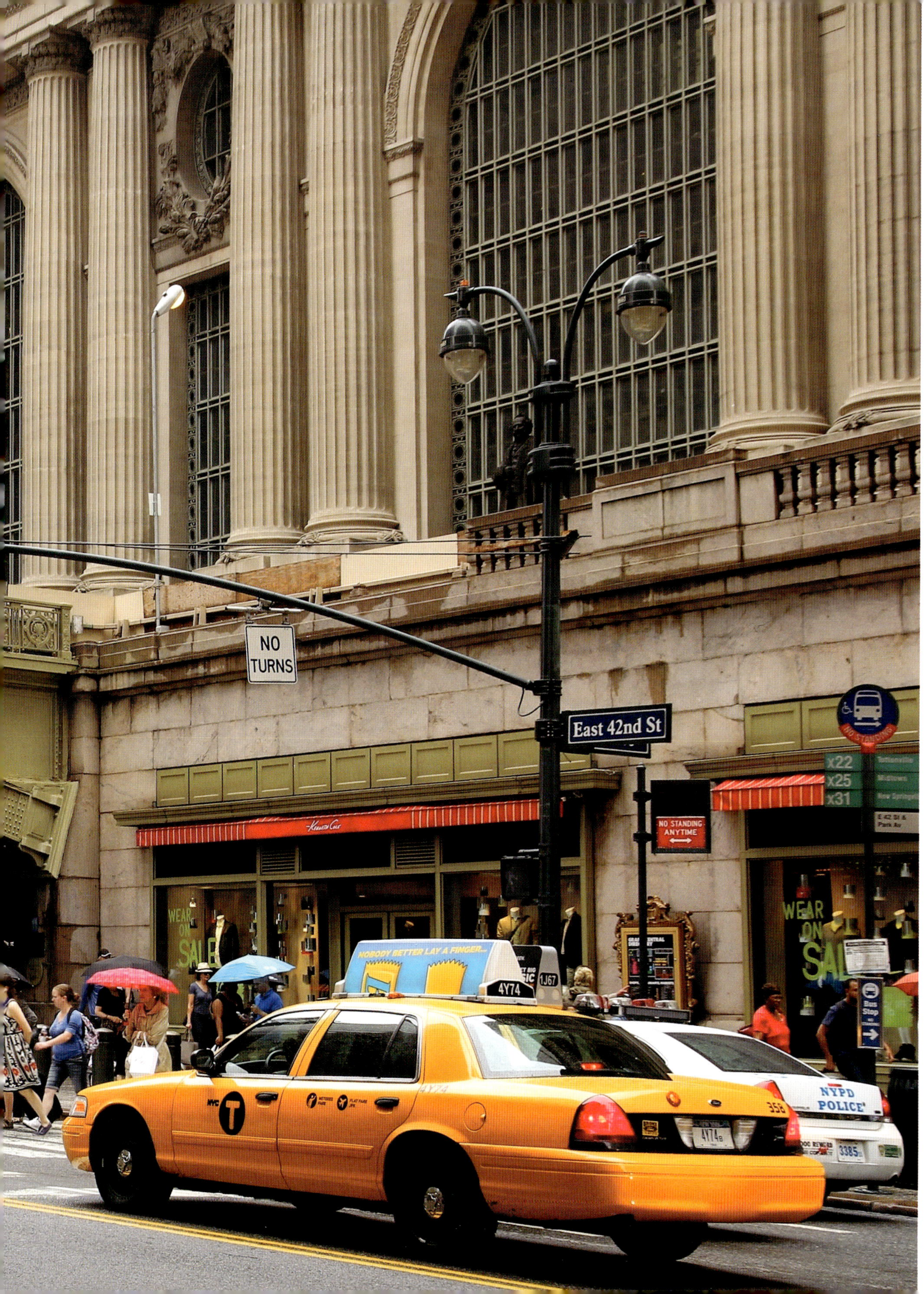

Grand Central Station, by sheer number of platforms alone, is the largest passenger rail facility in the world. More than just trains, the station also houses restaurants, shops, delis, and more, including an Oyster Bar, a Transit Museum, and an Apple Store.

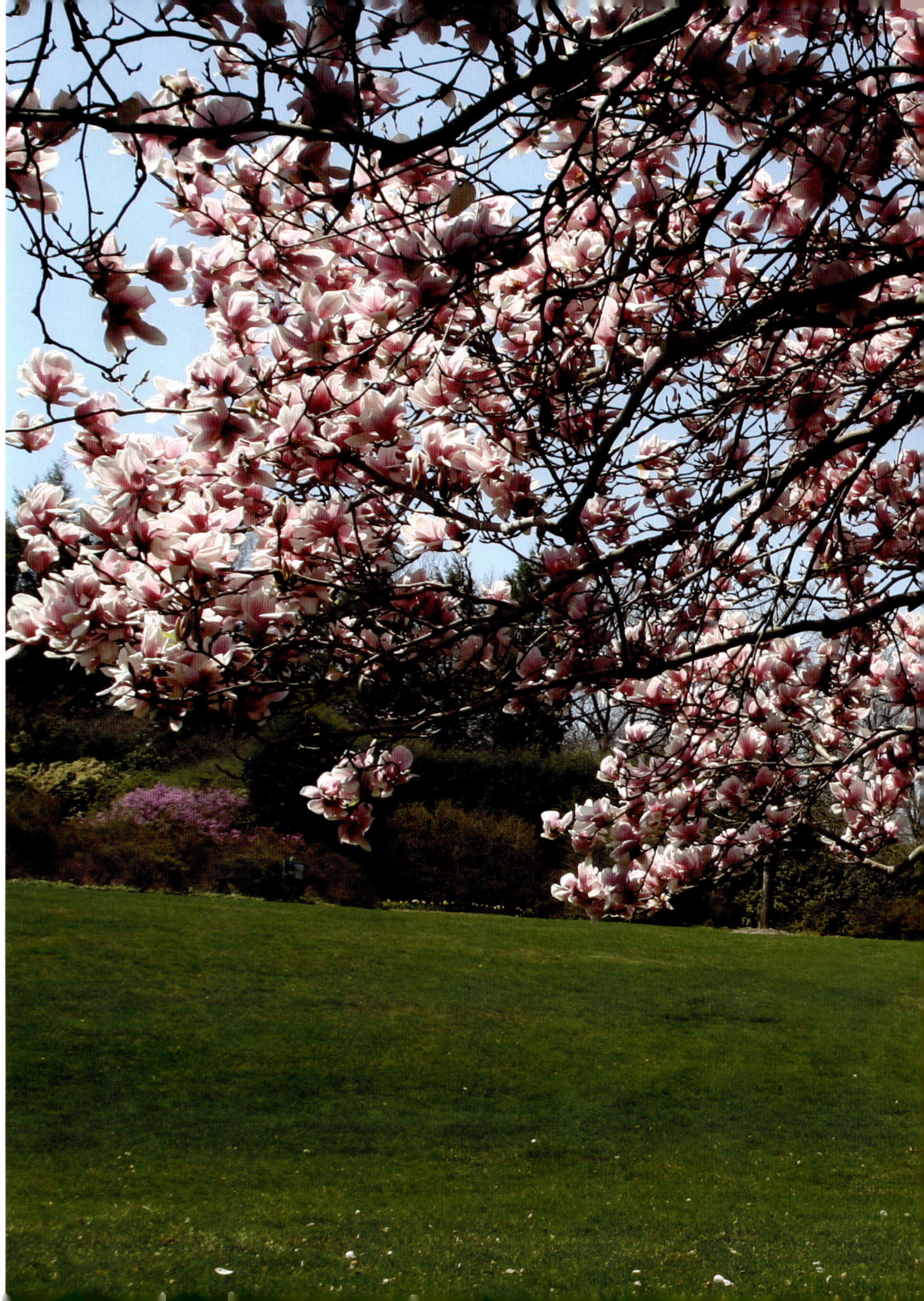

The journey continues north to Westchester. Here stands the main house of the Lasdon estate, built in 1933 and modeled after George Washington's home in Virginia. Today, the 234-acre Westchester estate encompasses gardens, arboretums, and memorials.

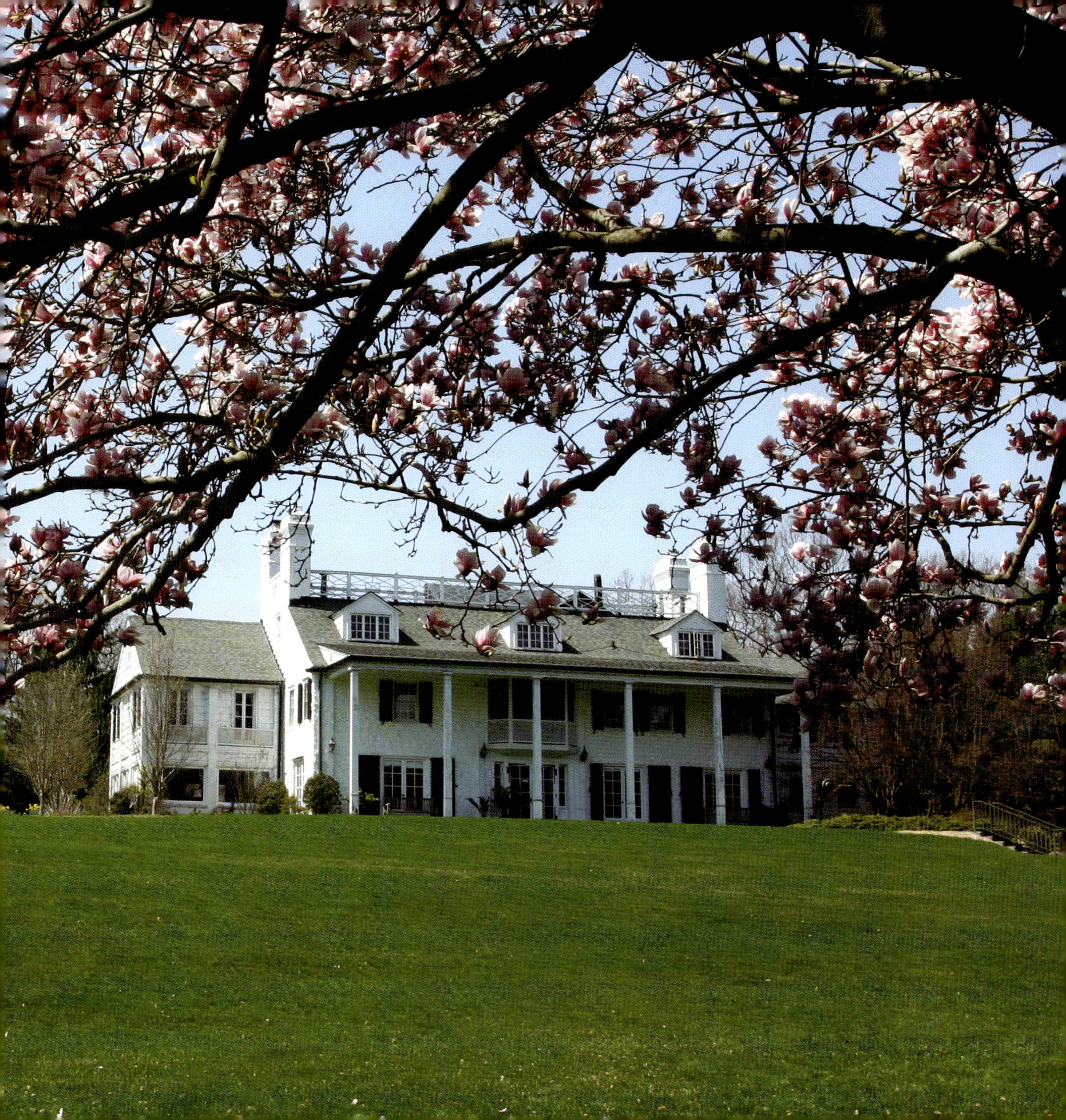

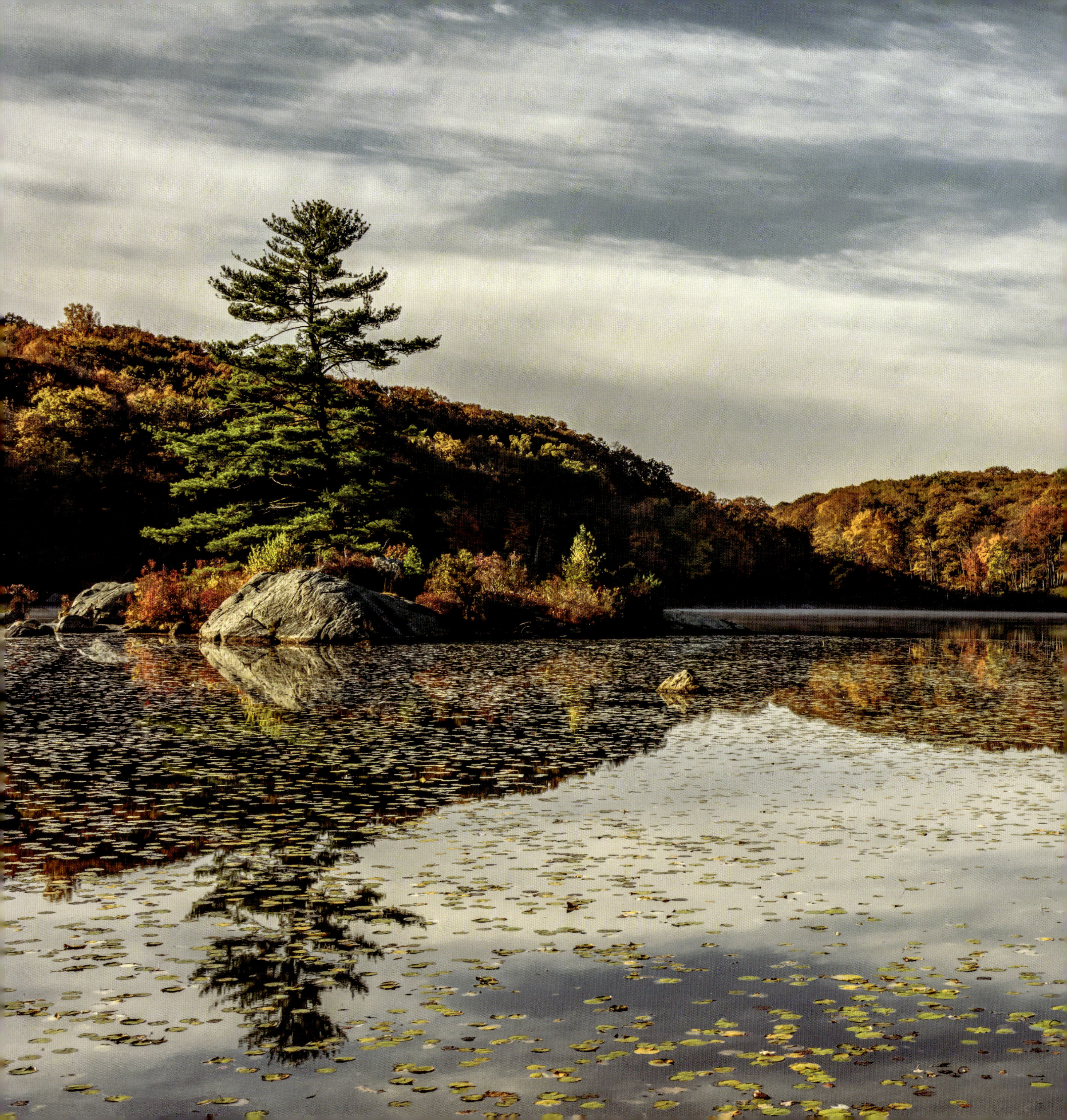

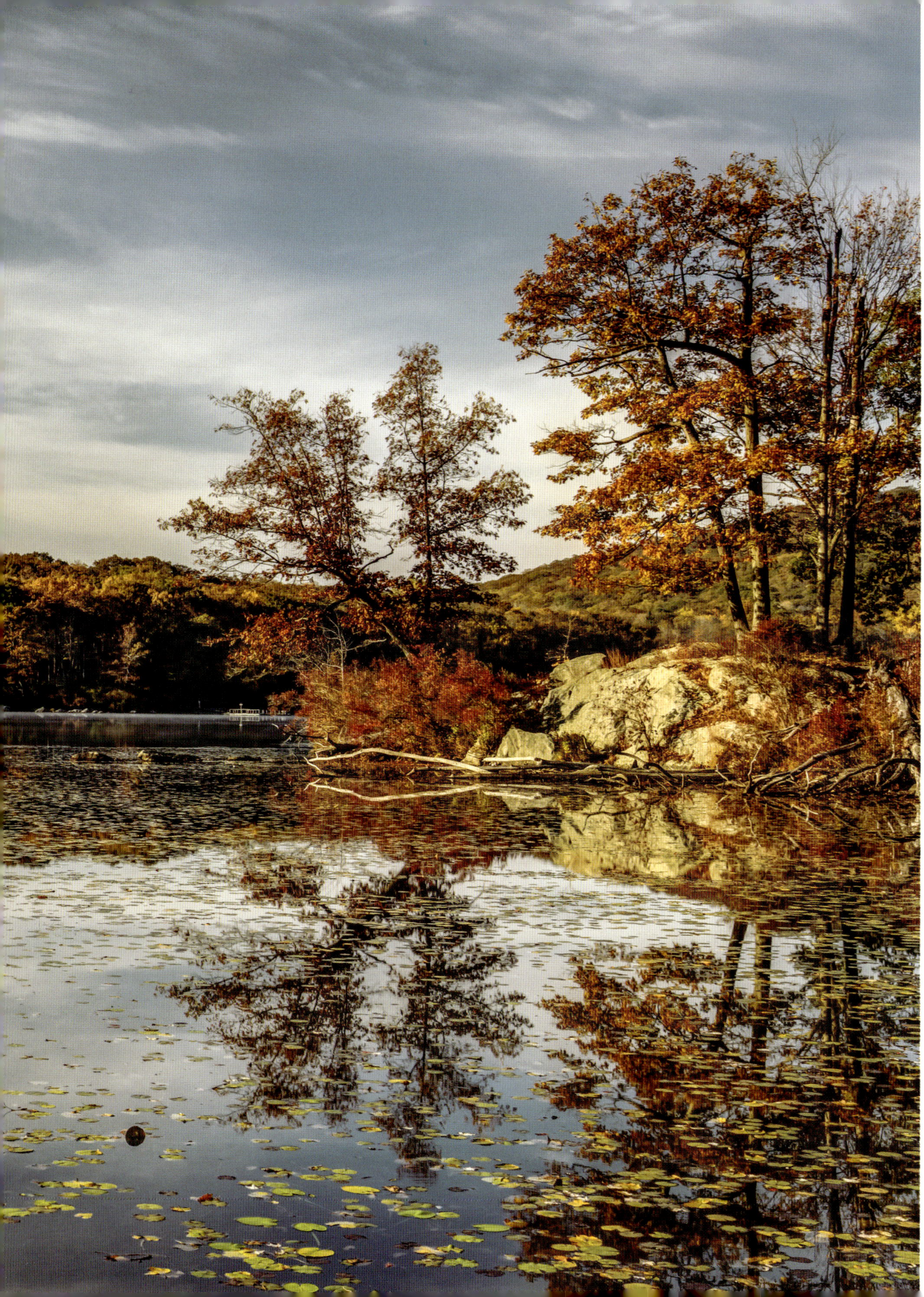

Autumn lights up the sugar maple trees with bright fall colors in Harriman State Park.

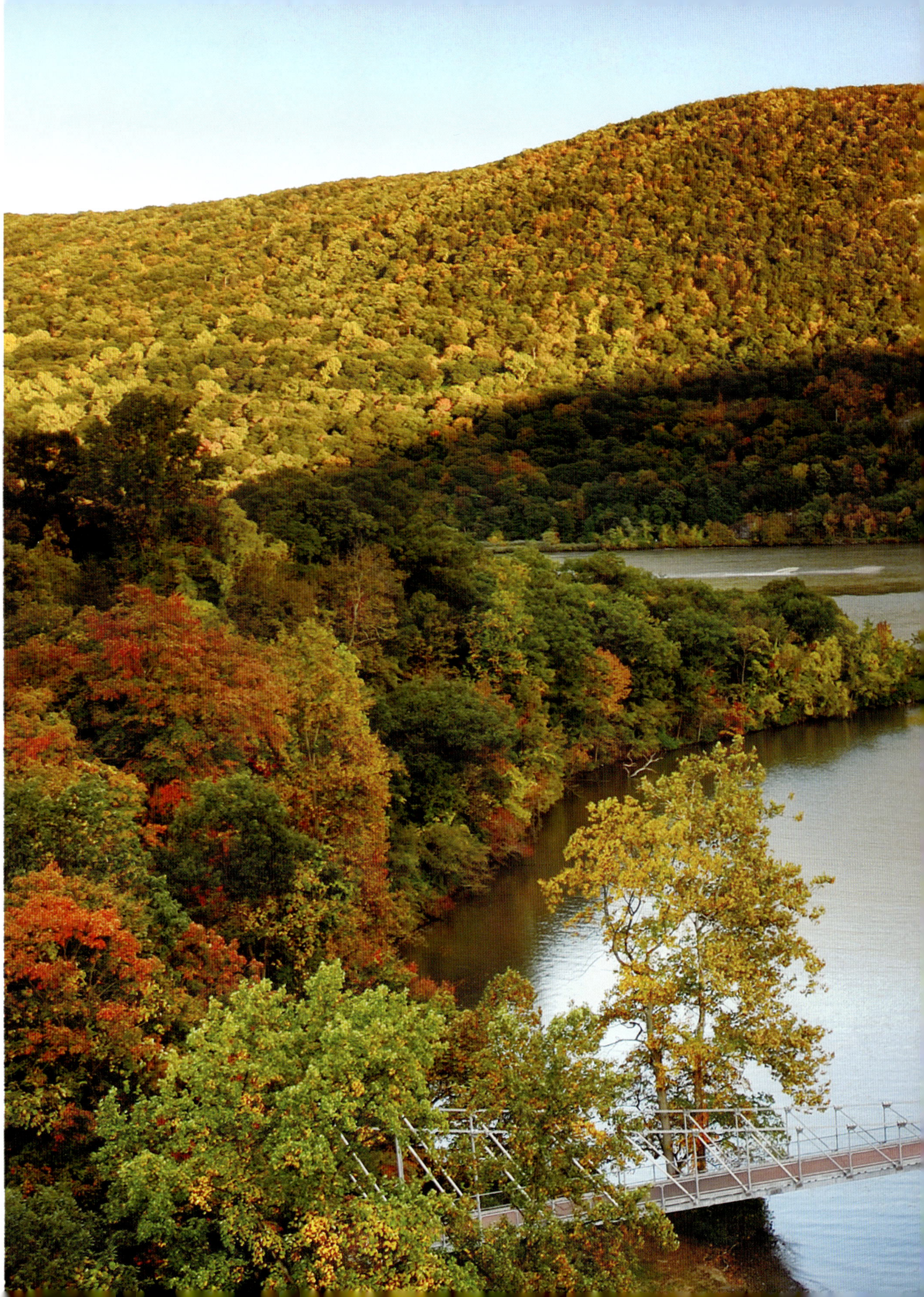

The lolling tree-lined hills of the Hudson River Valley have been embedded into American culture by Washington Irving's stories. The 315-mile watercourse is nicknamed "America's Rhine" for its picturesque natural beauty.

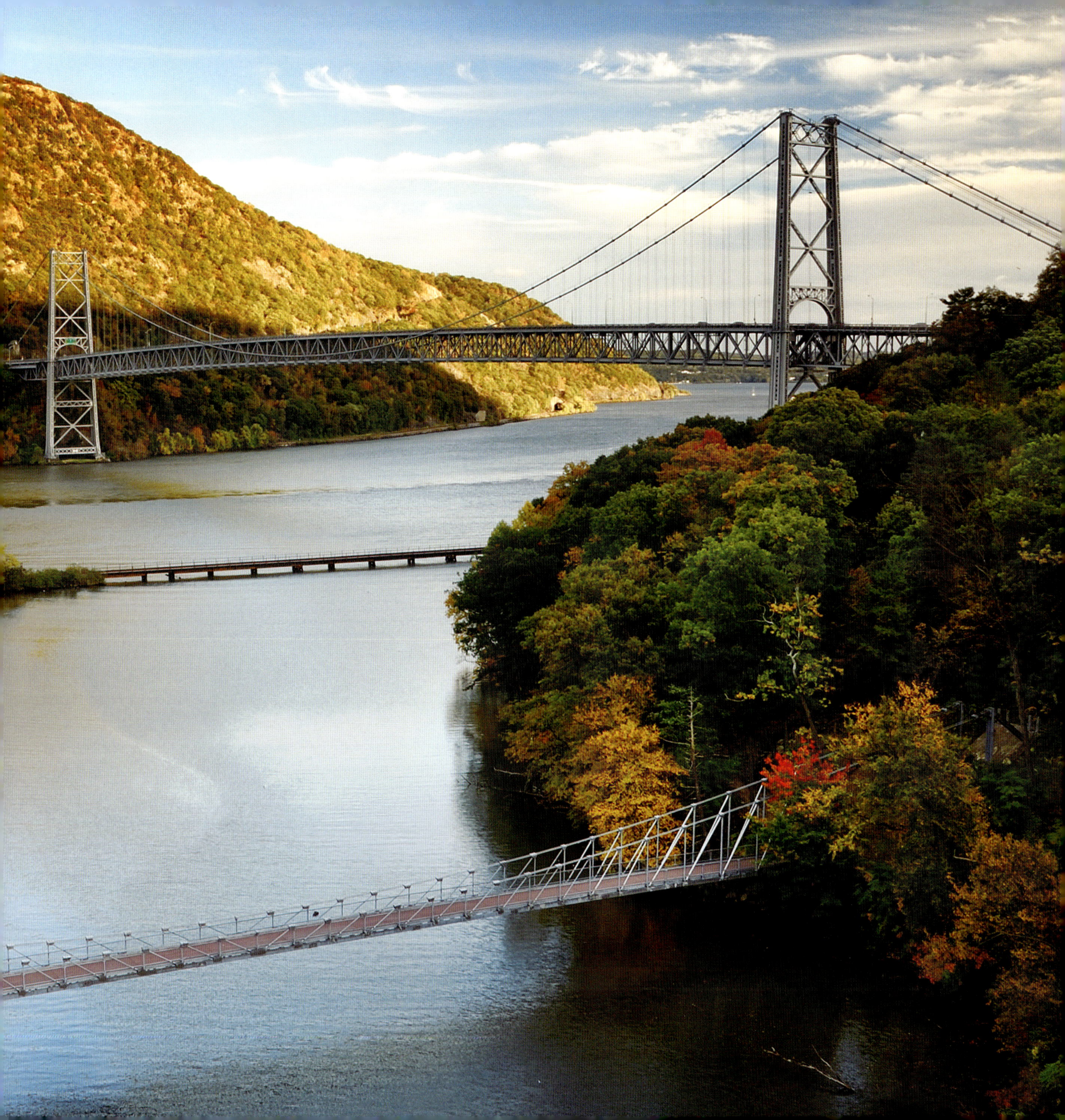

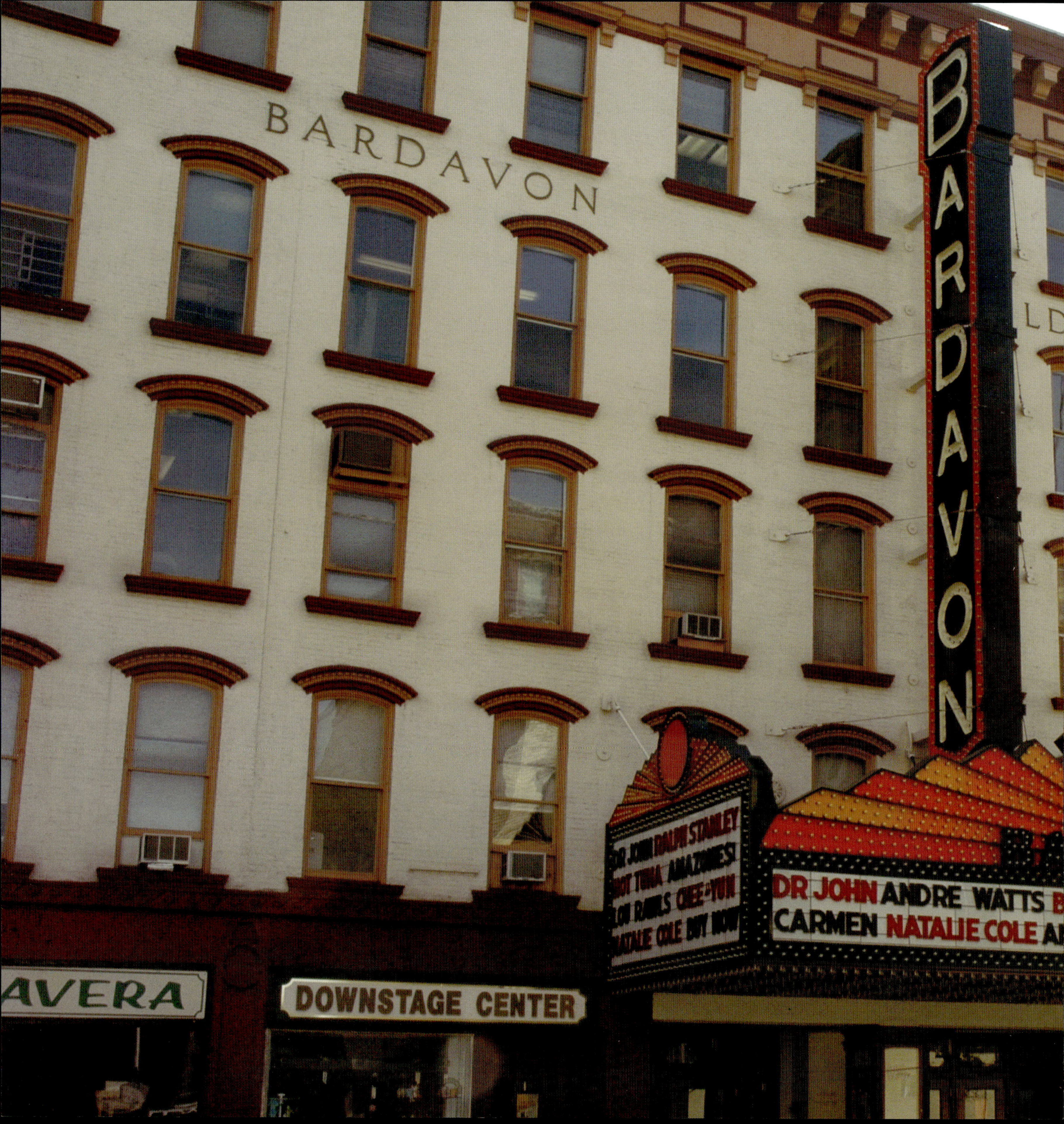
BARDAVON
BARDAVON
DR JOHN RALPH STANLEY
DR JOHN ANDRE WATTS
CARMEN NATALIE COLE
DOWNSTAGE CENTER

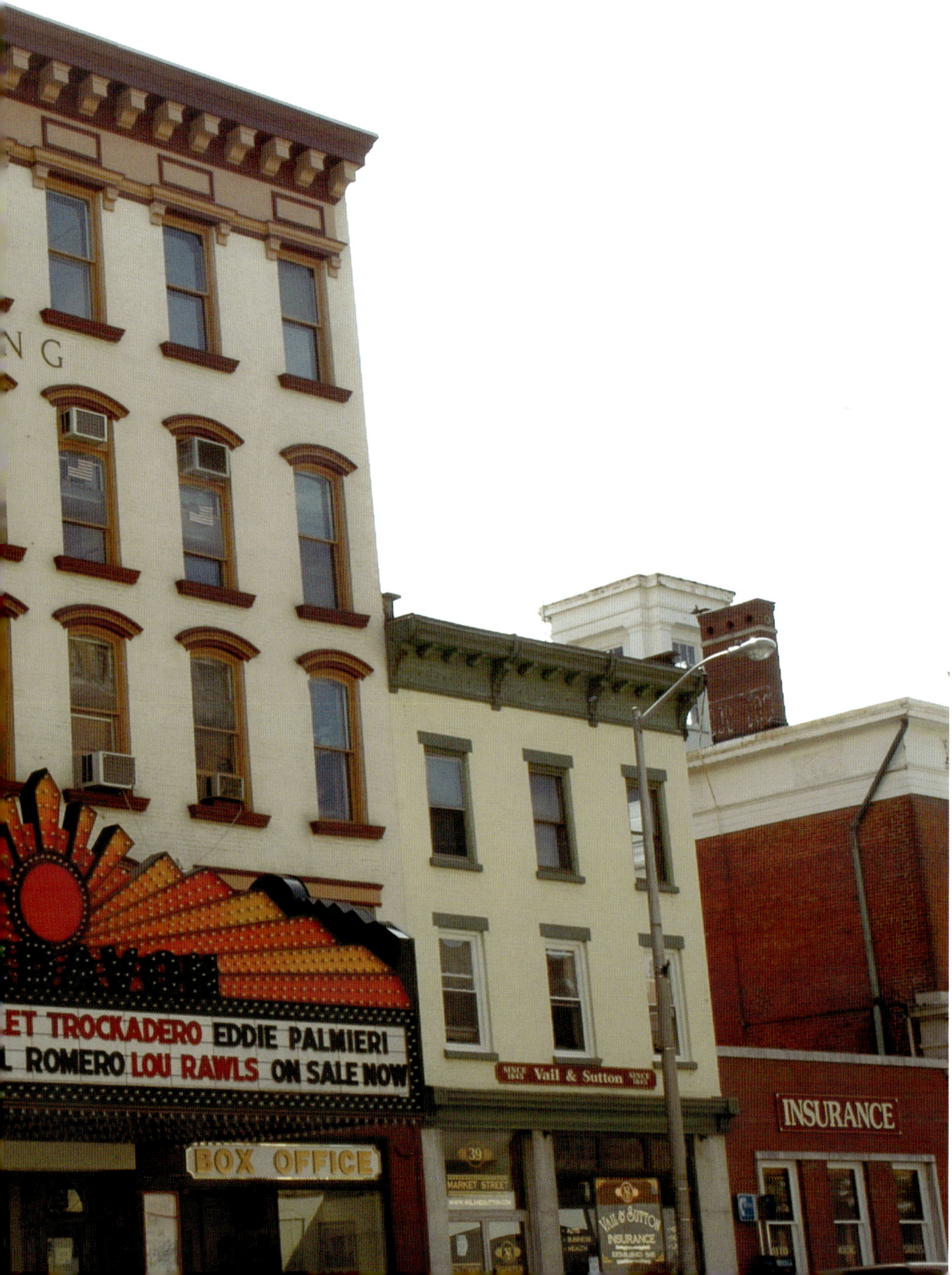

In operation as a performance venue since 1869, the Bardavon 1869 Opera House in Poughkeepsie has seen great American performers of all eras and disciplines, including Mark Twain, Martha Graham, Frank Sinatra, Dizzy Gillespie, and Patti Smith.

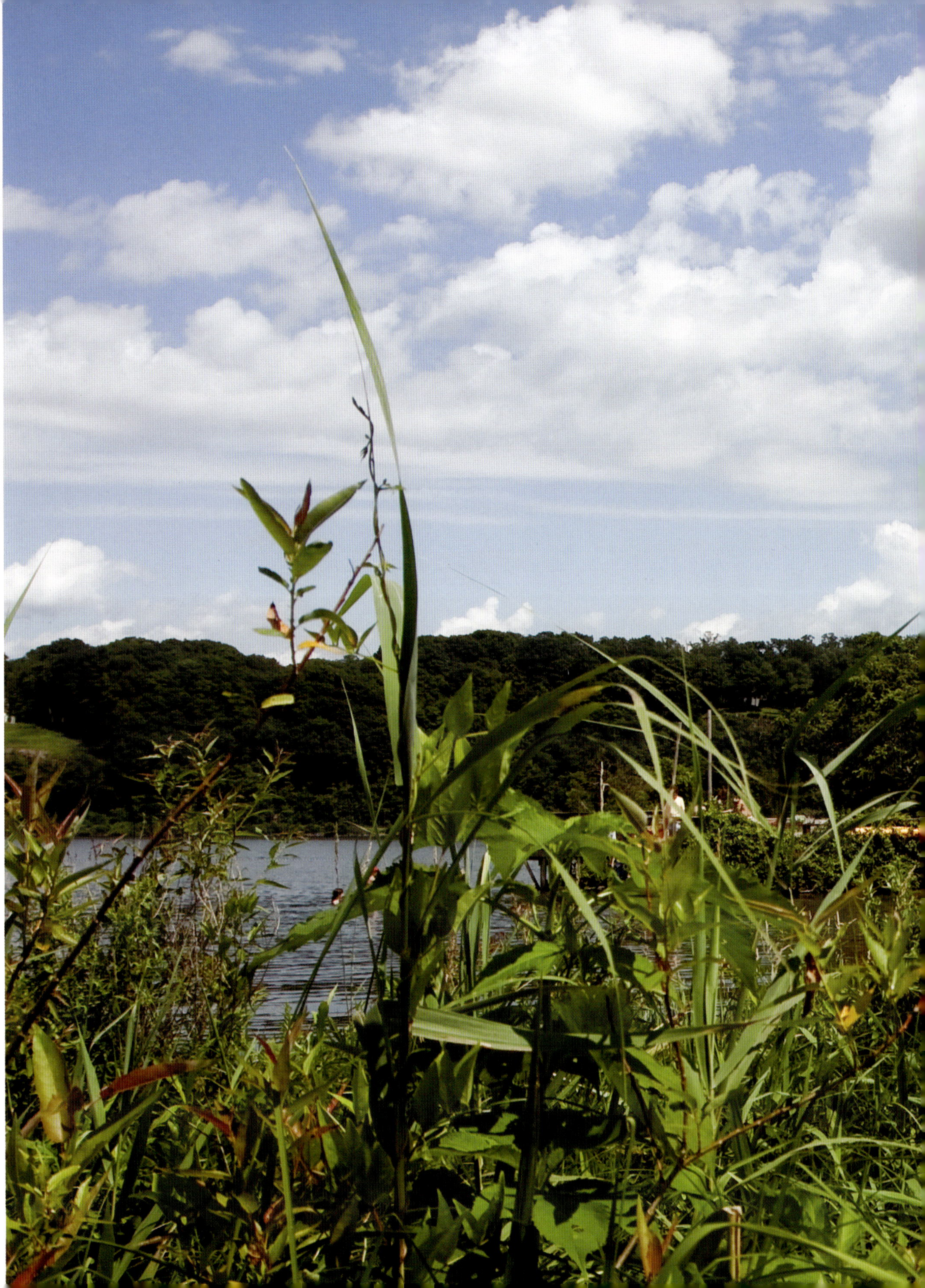

A red-brick beacon standing at the mouth of Esopus Creek, the Saugerties Lighthouse served as a venerable aid to navigation along the Hudson River. Though falling into disrepair, the now-restored historic lighthouse runs a bed and breakfast, museum, and nature trail.

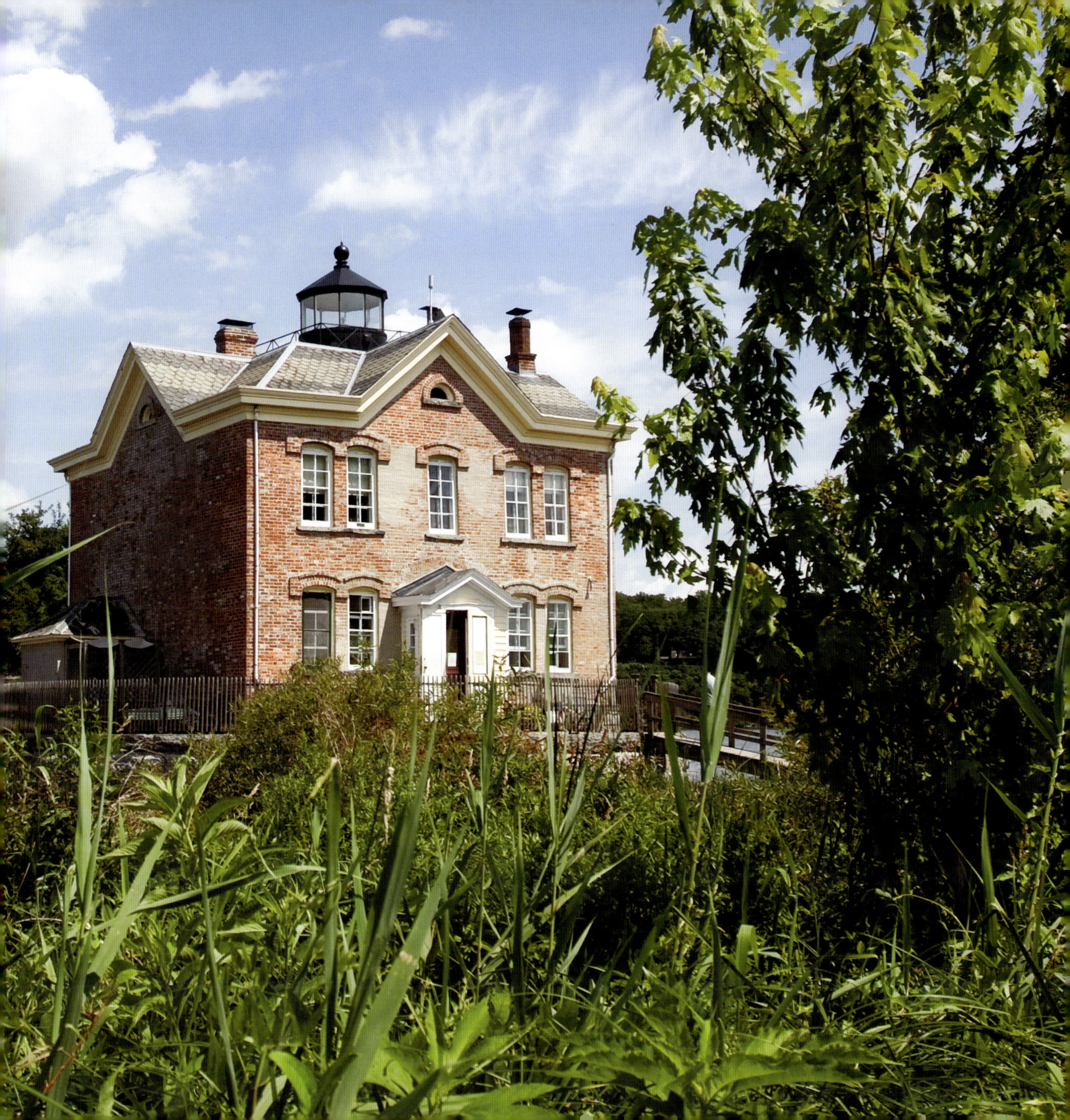

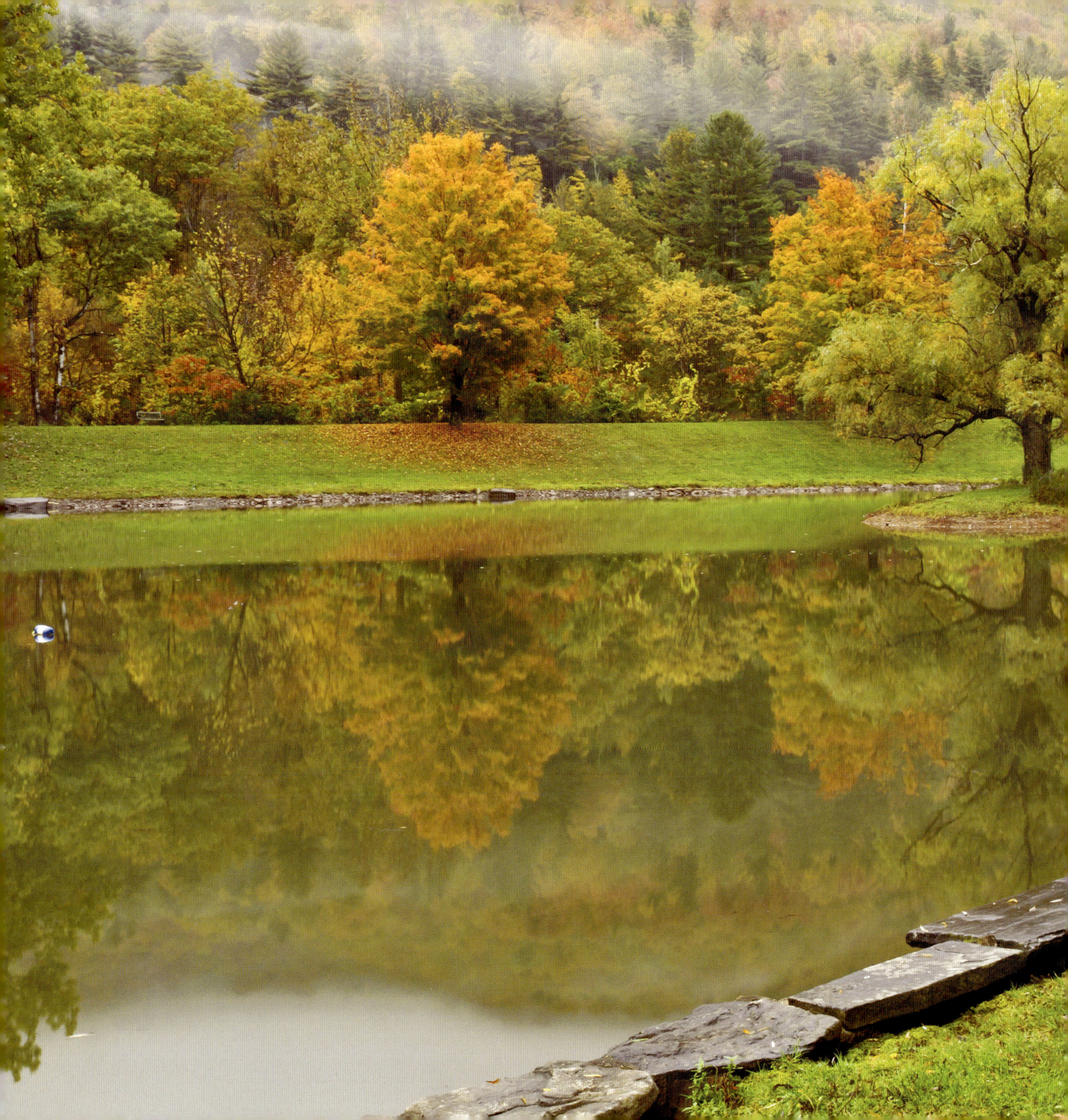

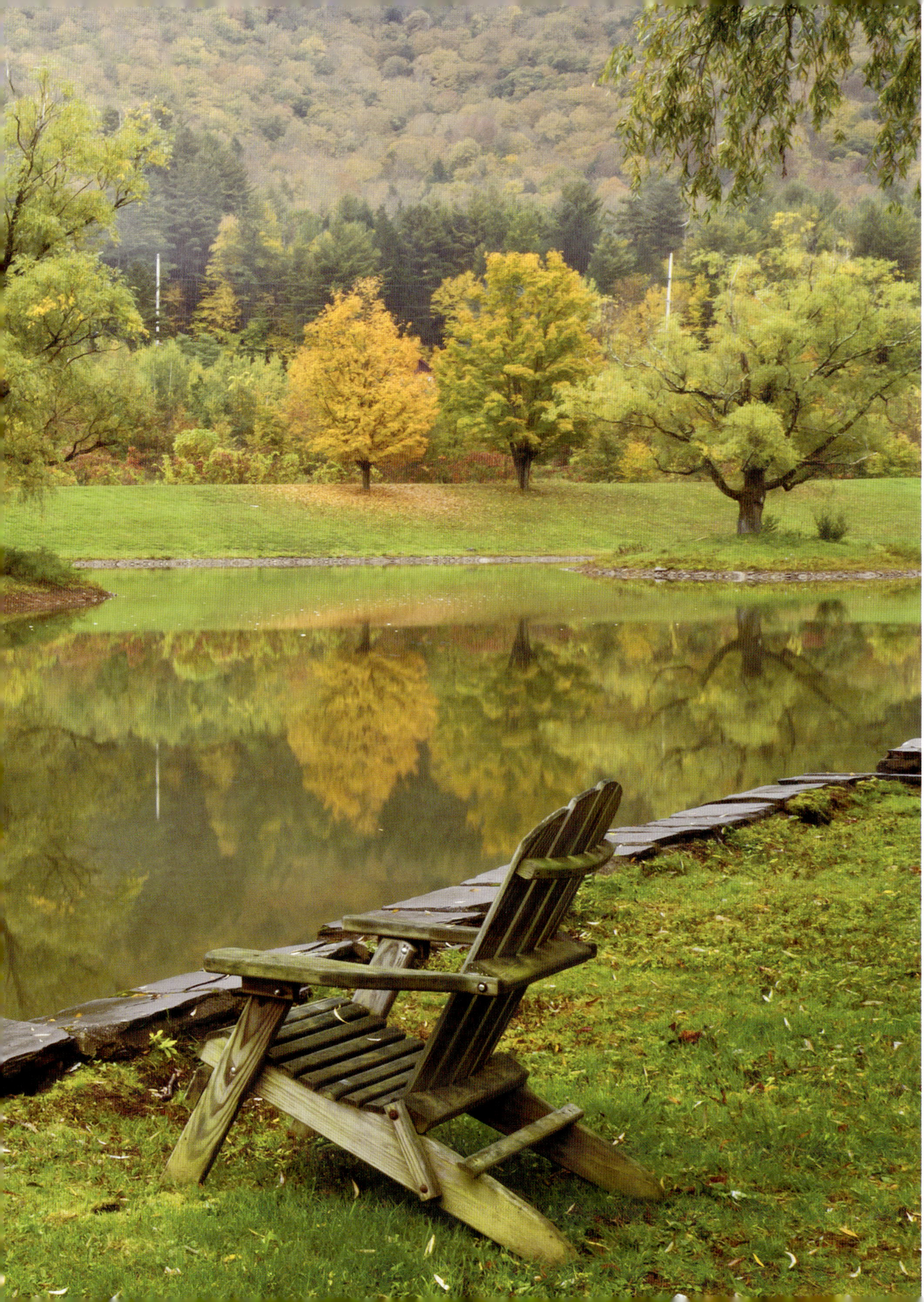

Roughly a mere 100 miles from New York City, the Catskills Mountains were a favored destination for urban vacationers in the mid 20th century. Its many resorts gave countless opportunities to "Borscht Belt comics," kickstarting the careers of notables such as Henny Youngman, Milton Berle, and Rodney Dangerfield.

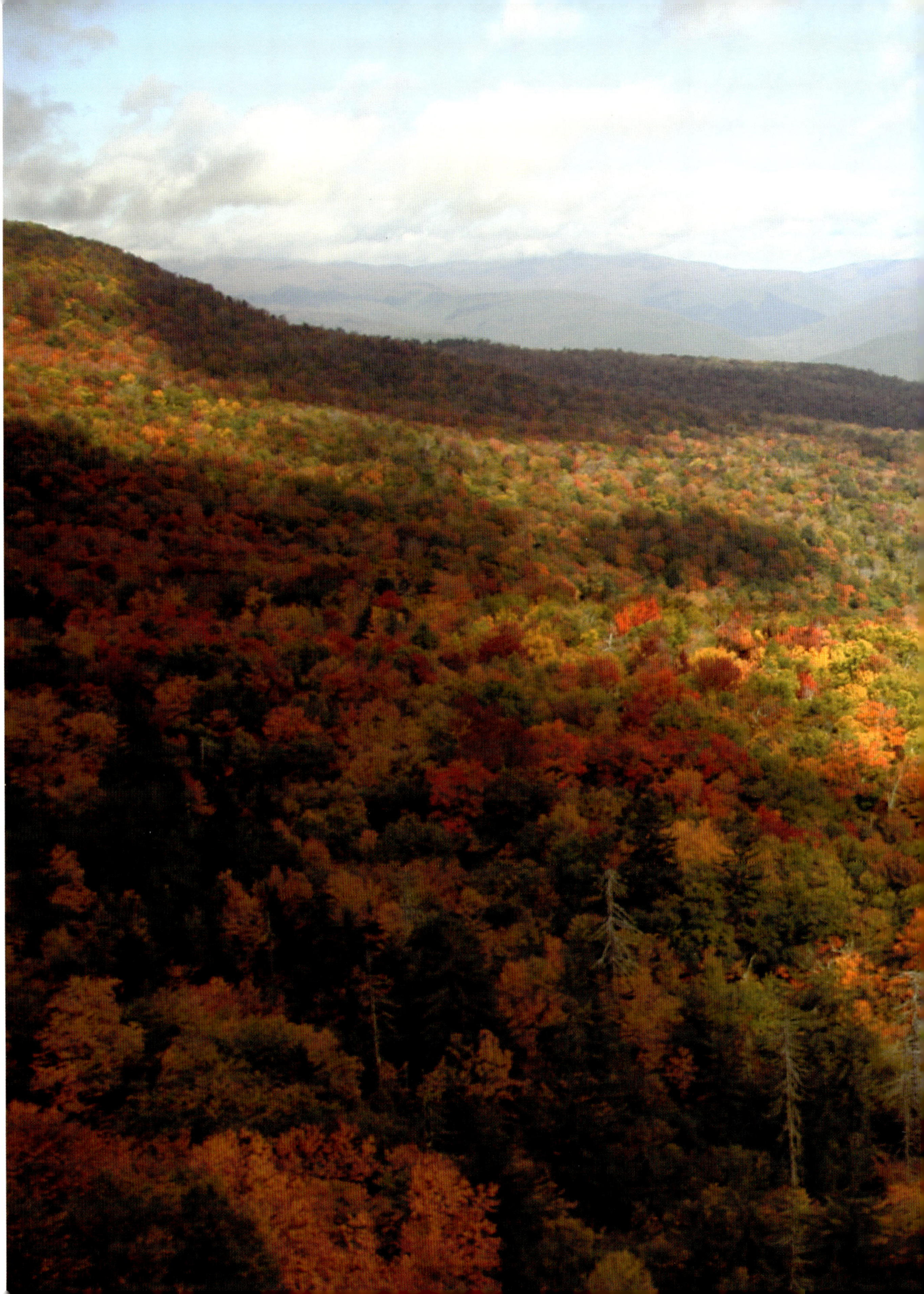

The spectacular fall foliage and romantic landscapes in the Catskills served as an inspiring setting for many Hudson River School paintings.

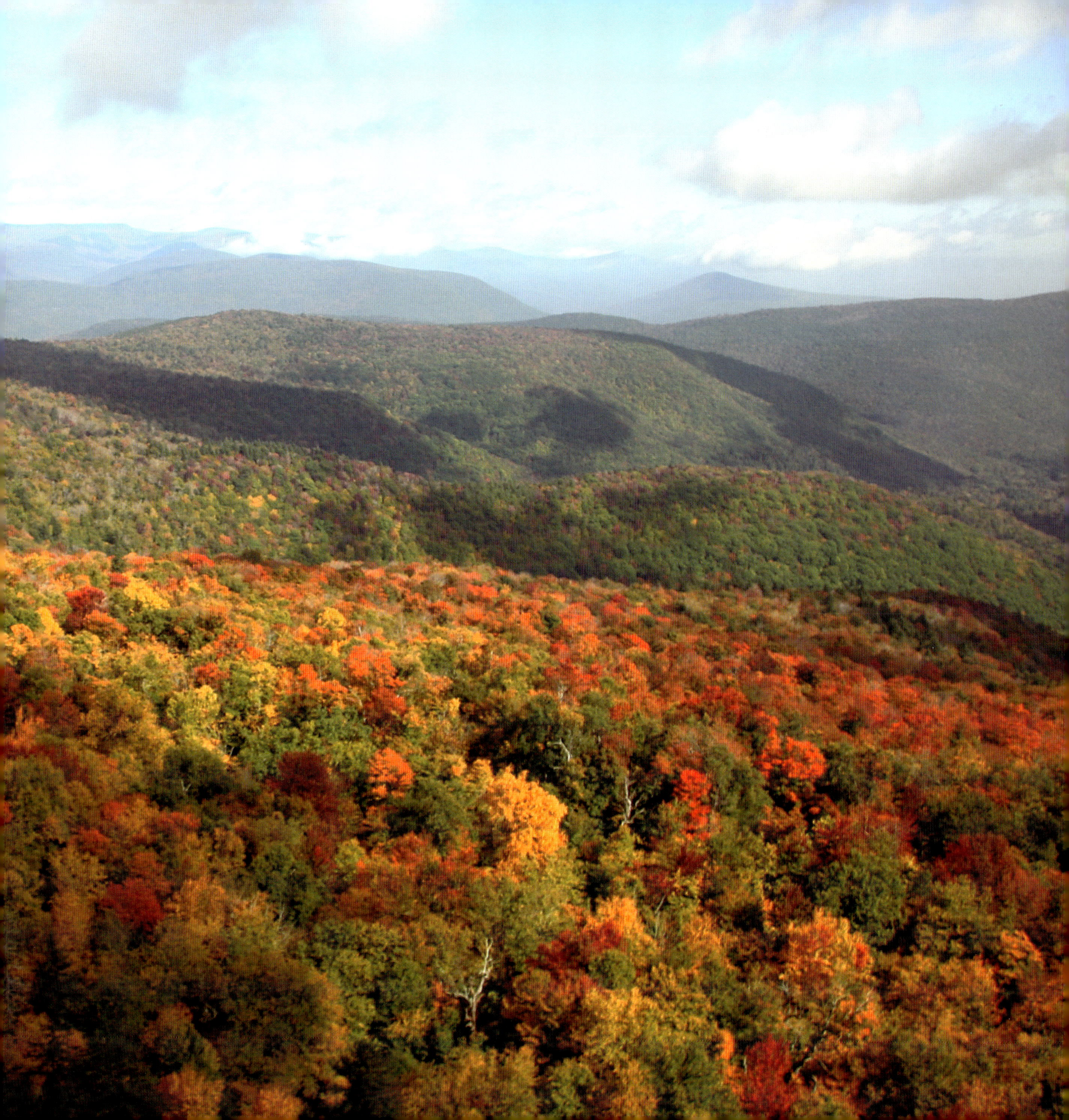

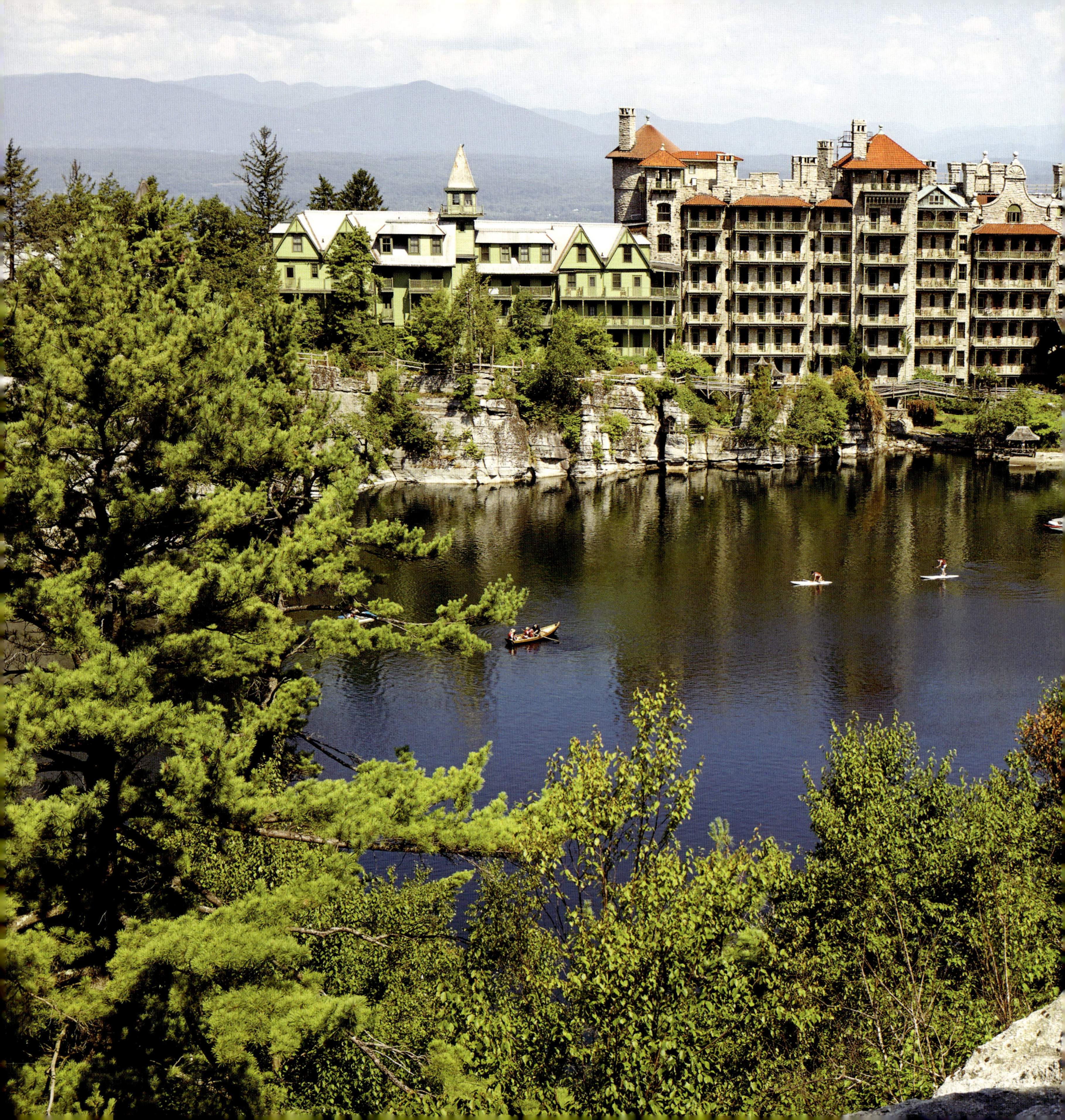

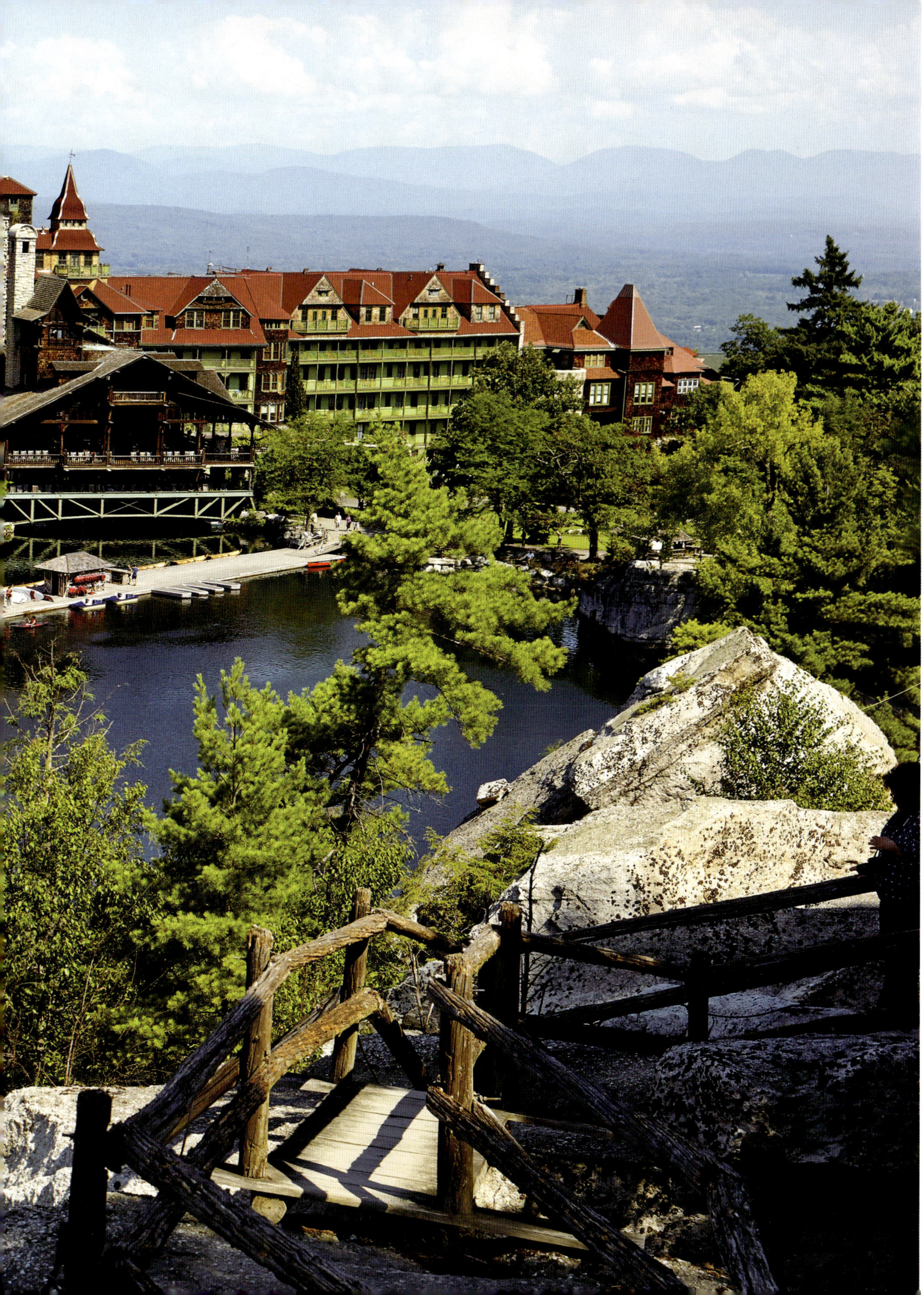

The Mohonk Mountain House near New Paltz began as a small resort built by Quaker twin brothers Albert and Alfred Smiley in the 1870s. The spa and preserves became so popular that it was enlarged many times to the sprawling and monumental size it is today.

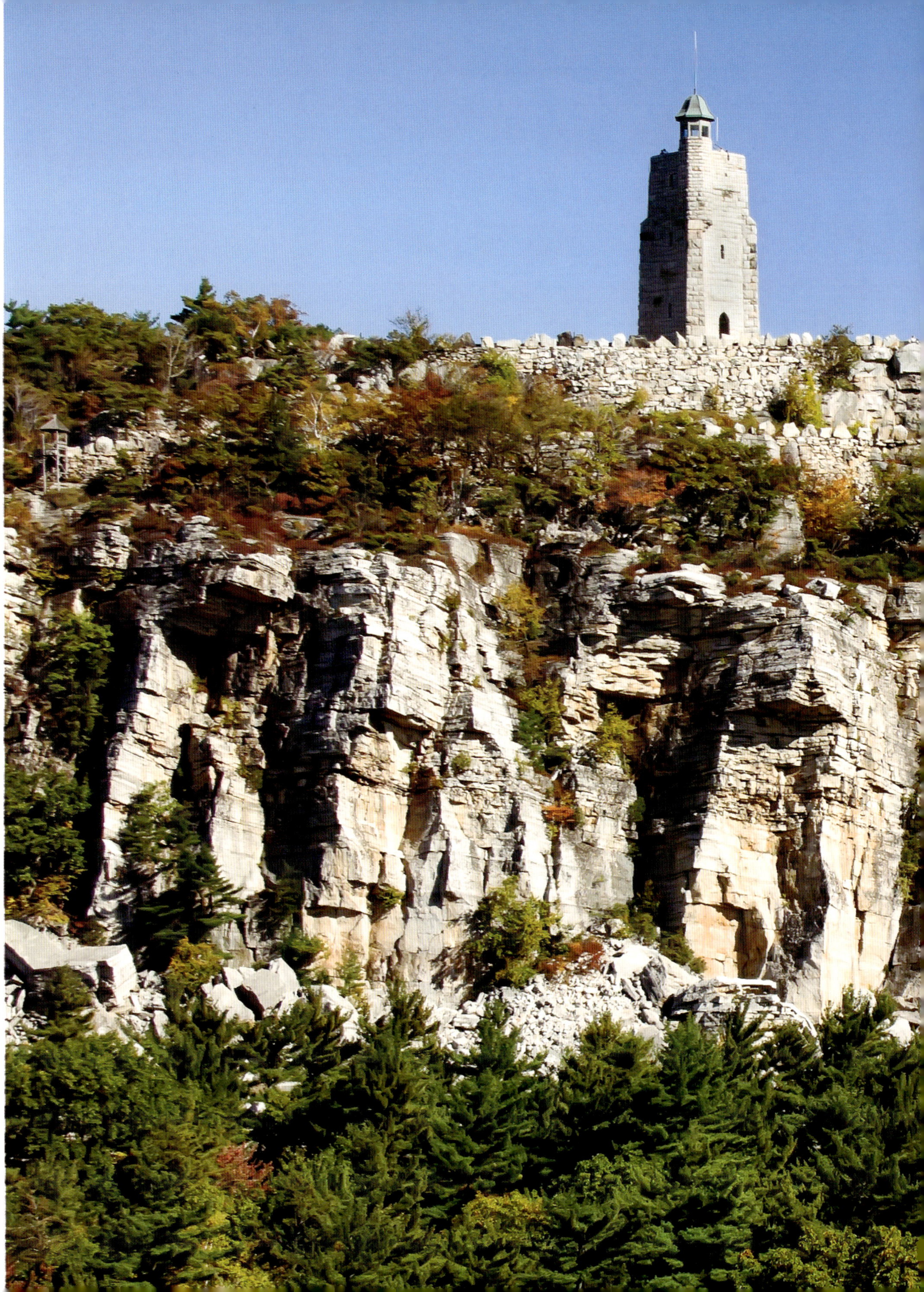

An hour-long hike through towering crags, limestone crevices, and boulder fields traces the shoreline of Mohonk Lake and ends with the vista from the memorial Skytop Tower. From this mountain peak, intrepid climbers can view the craggy Shawangunk Ridge.

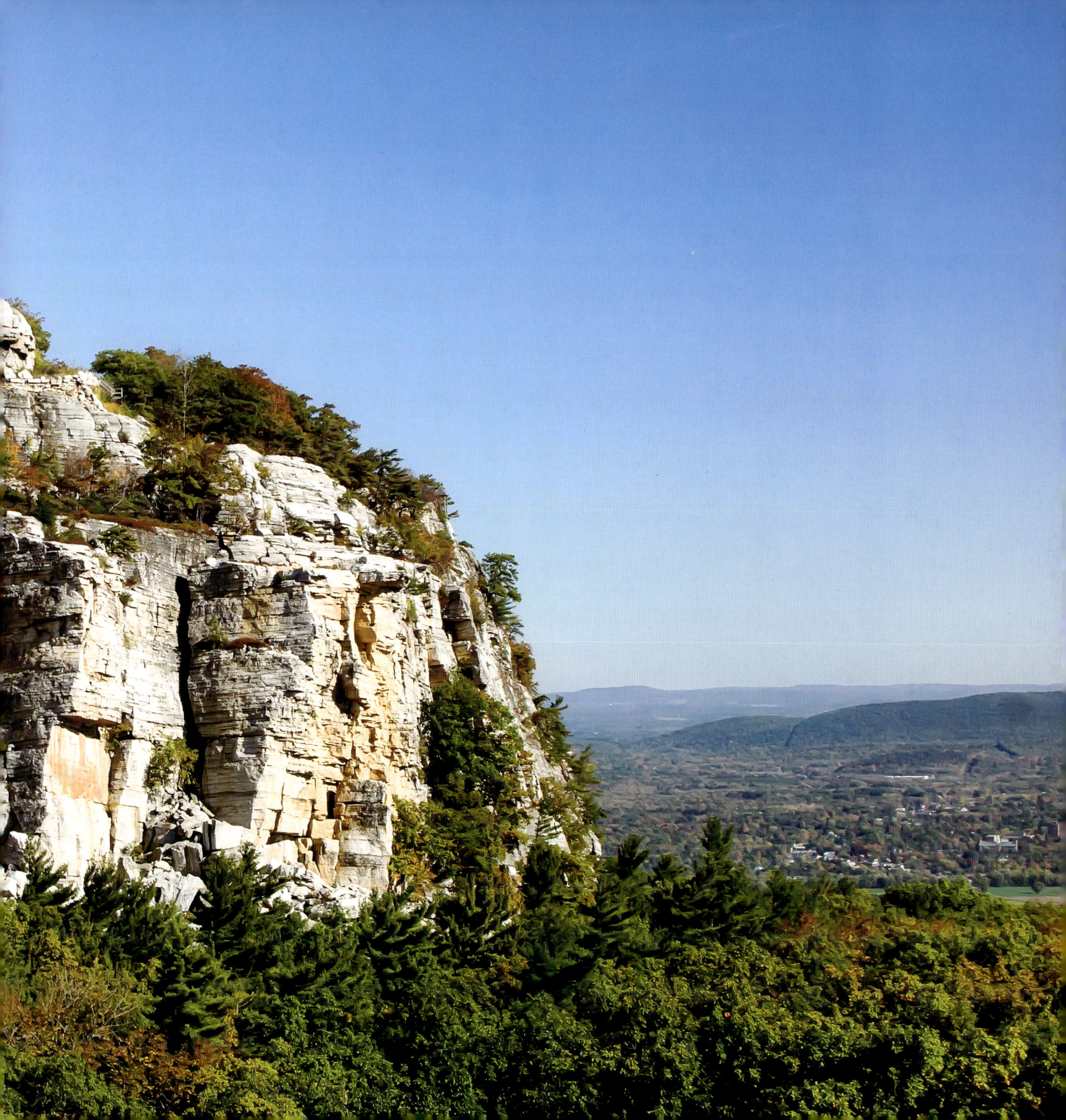

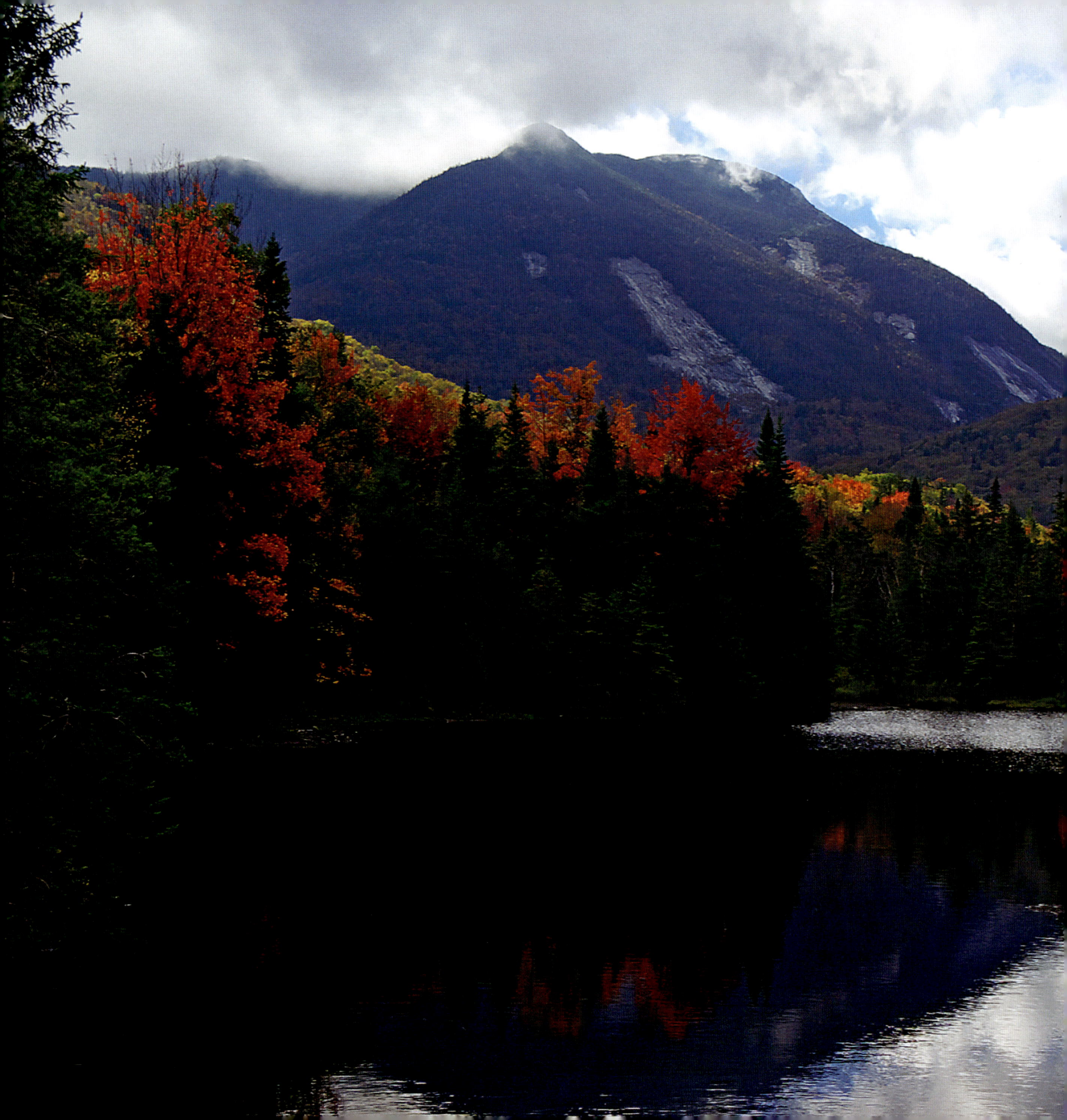

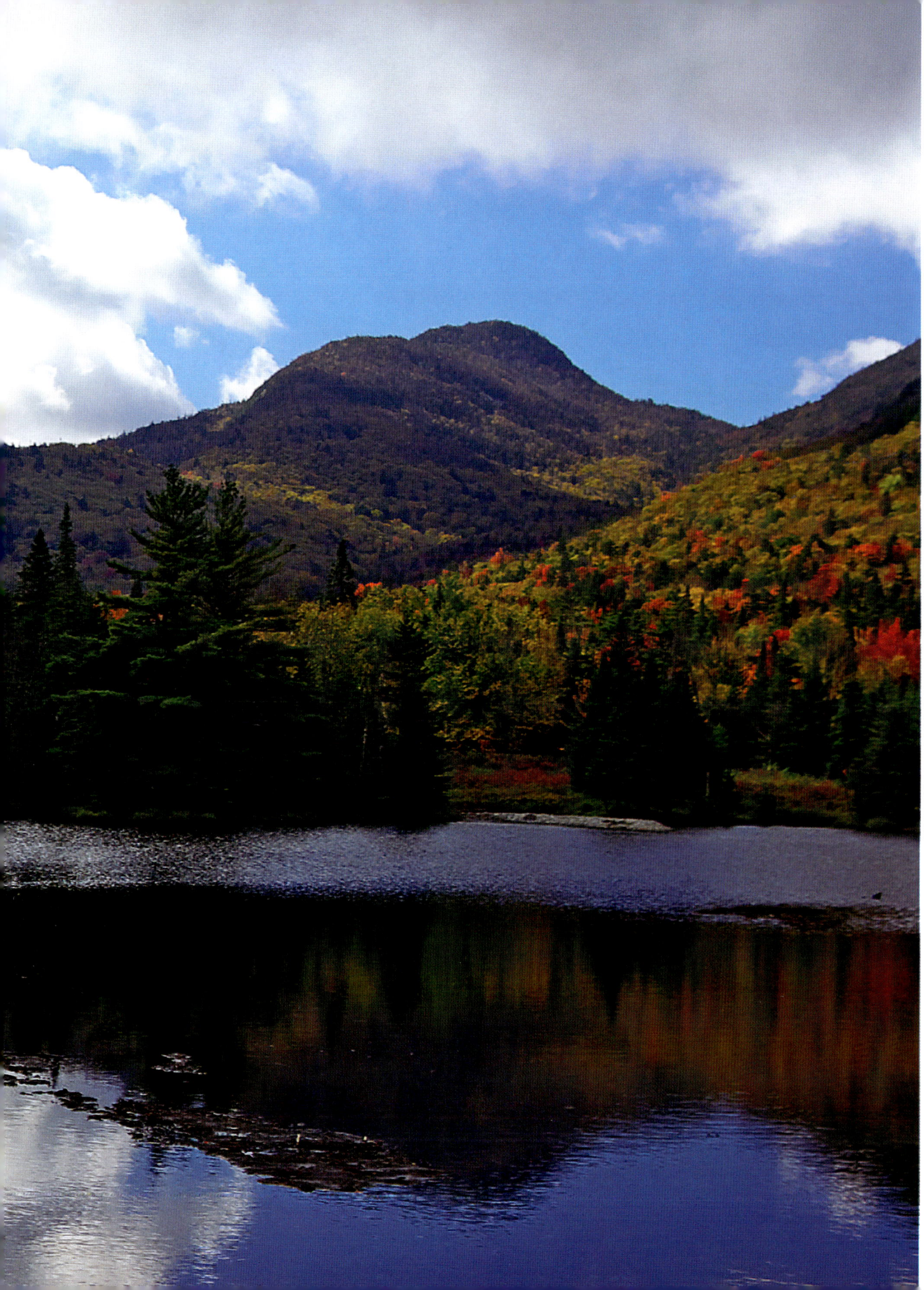

Adirondack State Park encompasses an area roughly the size of Massachusetts; running through the park is its namesake, the Adirondack Mountains. A popular mountaineering goal is to join the "Forty Sixers" club, by climbing the 46 highest peaks.

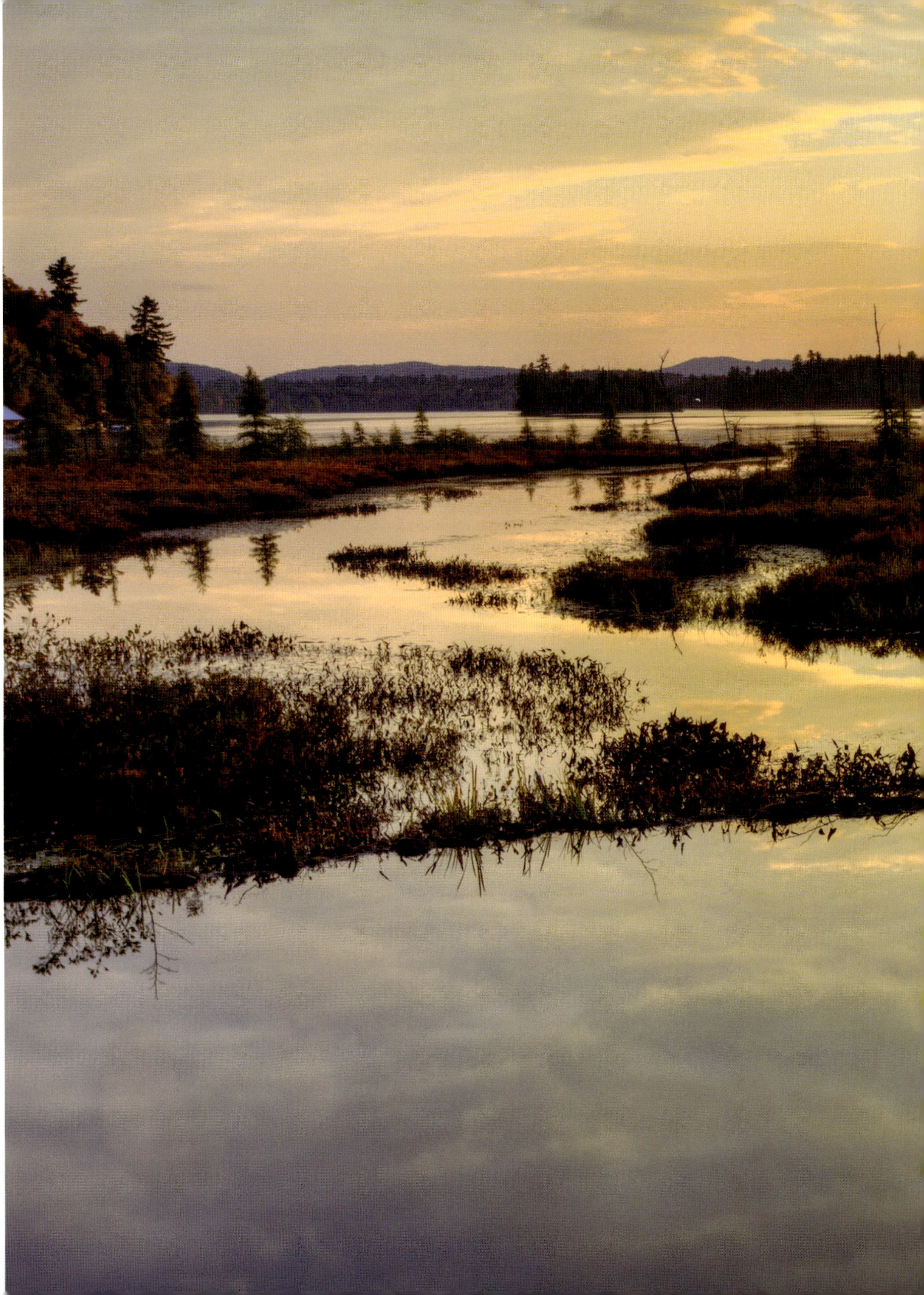

A sunrise is reflected in Brown's Tract Inlet off Raquette Lake. Nearly 2.3 million acres of the Adirondacks have been declared "forever wild" and are a constitutionally protected forest preserve.

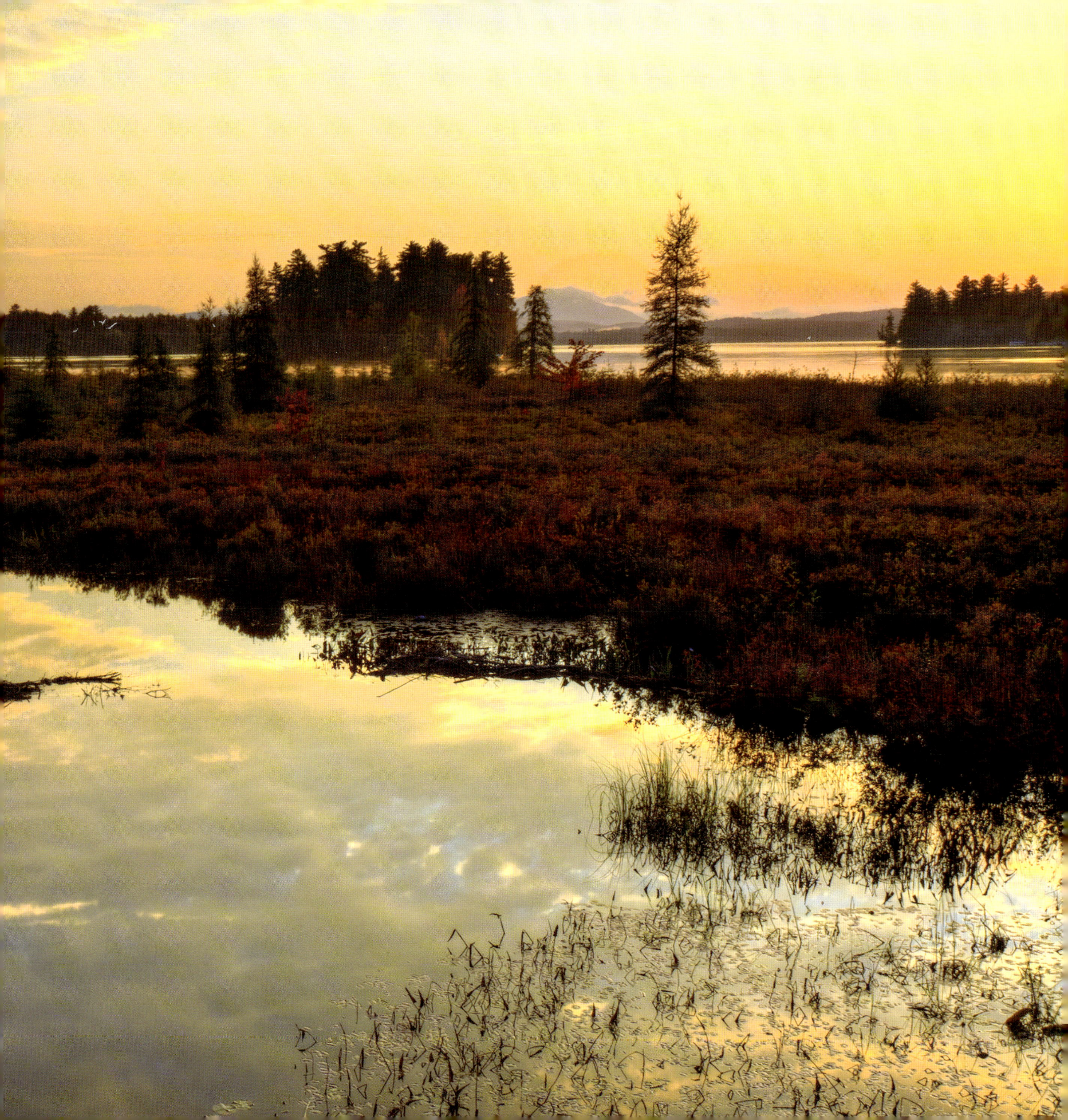

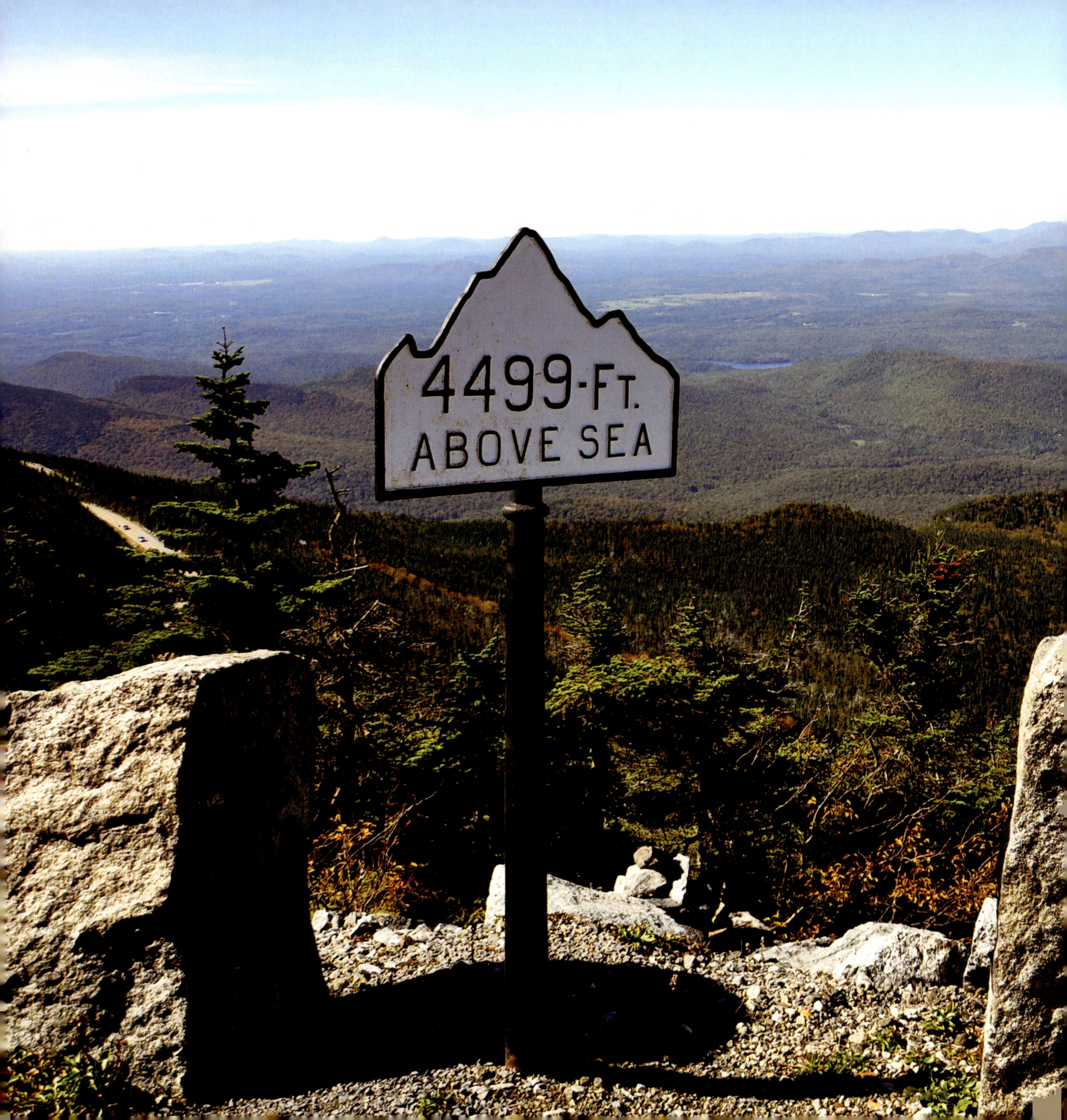
4499-Ft.
ABOVE SEA

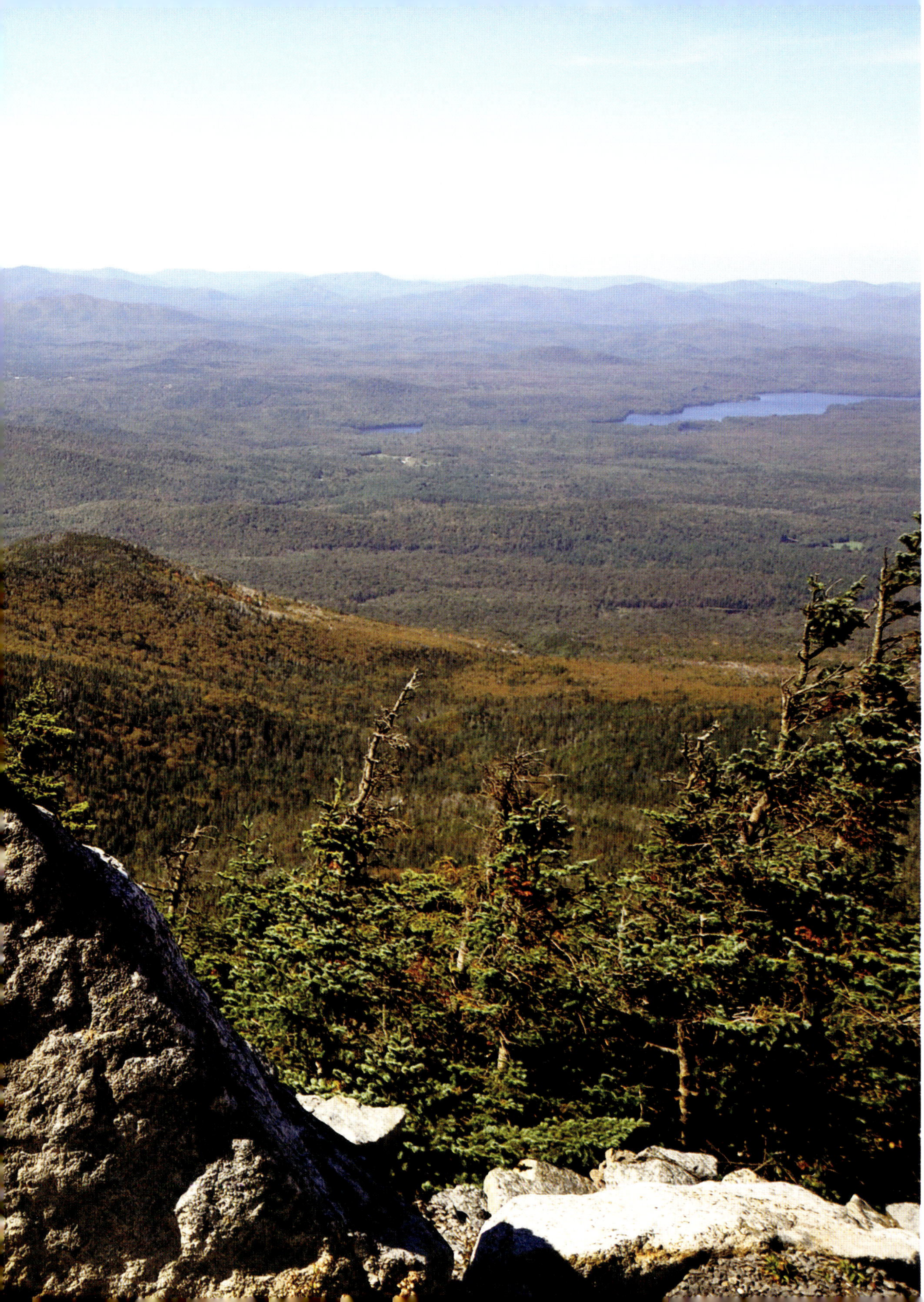

Set apart from the rest of the Adirondacks is Whiteface Mountain. From the halfway point, a clear day offers glimpses into neighboring states; from the summit one can even see the skyscrapers of Montreal in Canada.

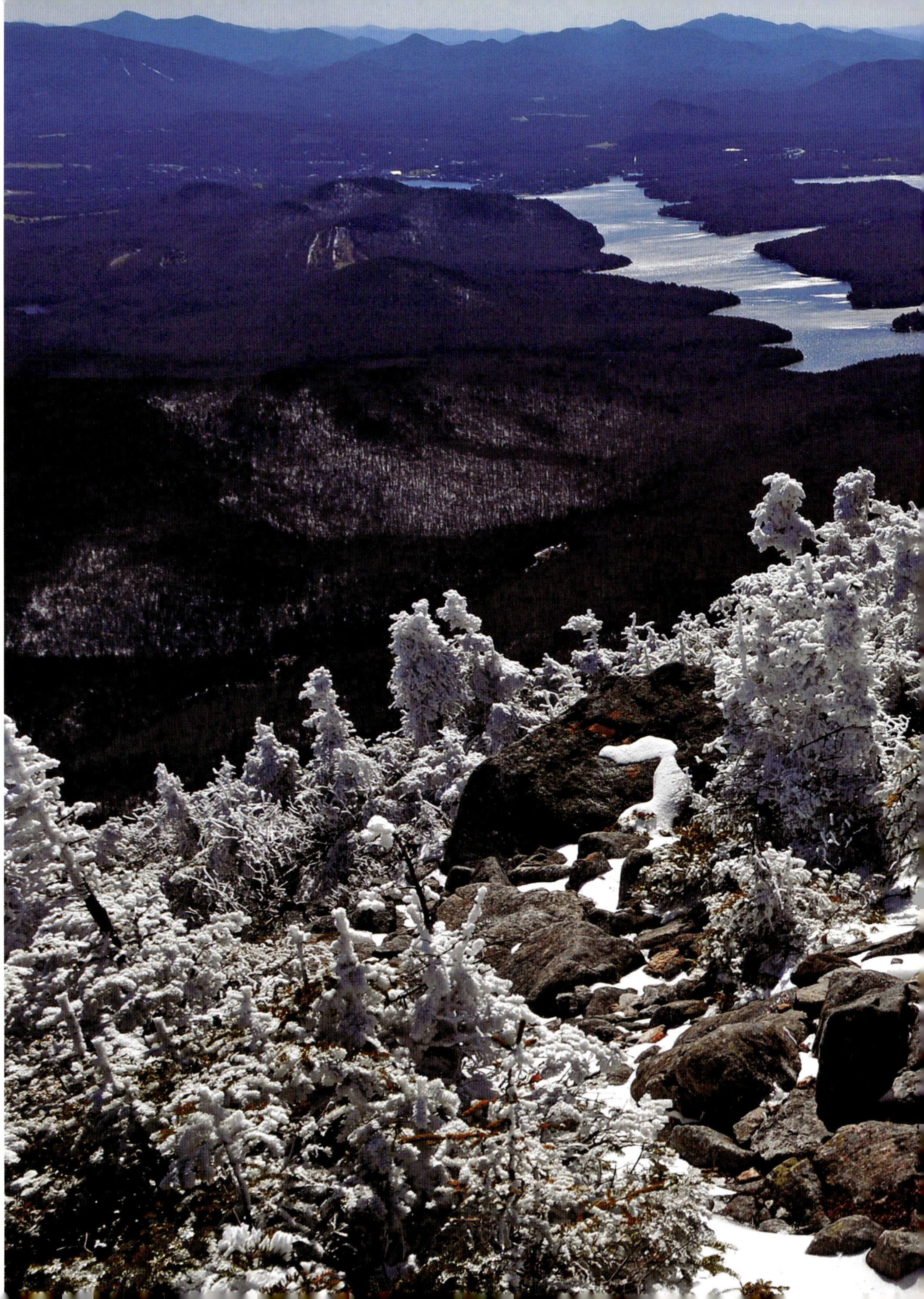

Looking down from the summit of Whiteface Mountain, the calm, shallow waters of Lake Placid come into view.

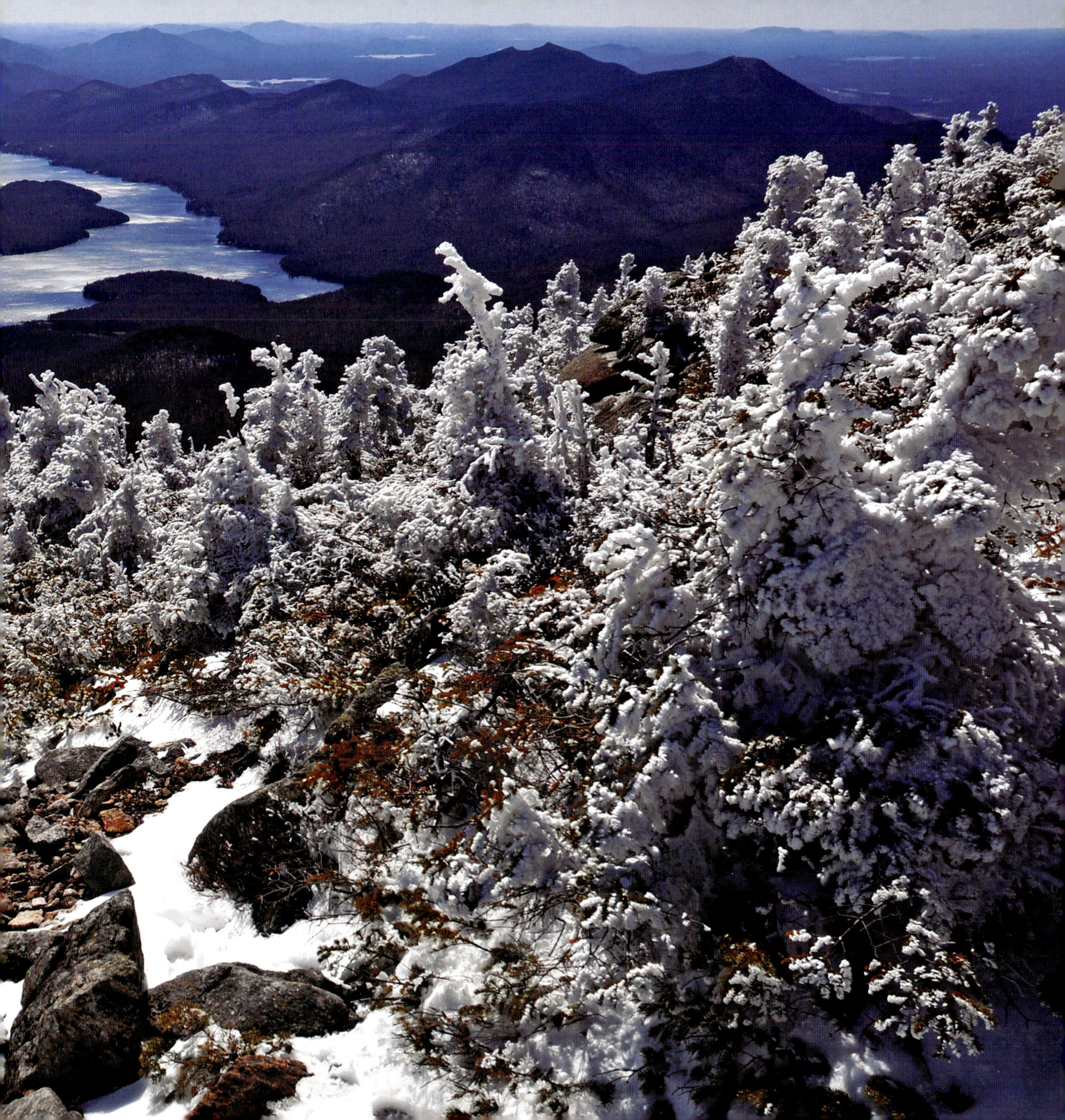

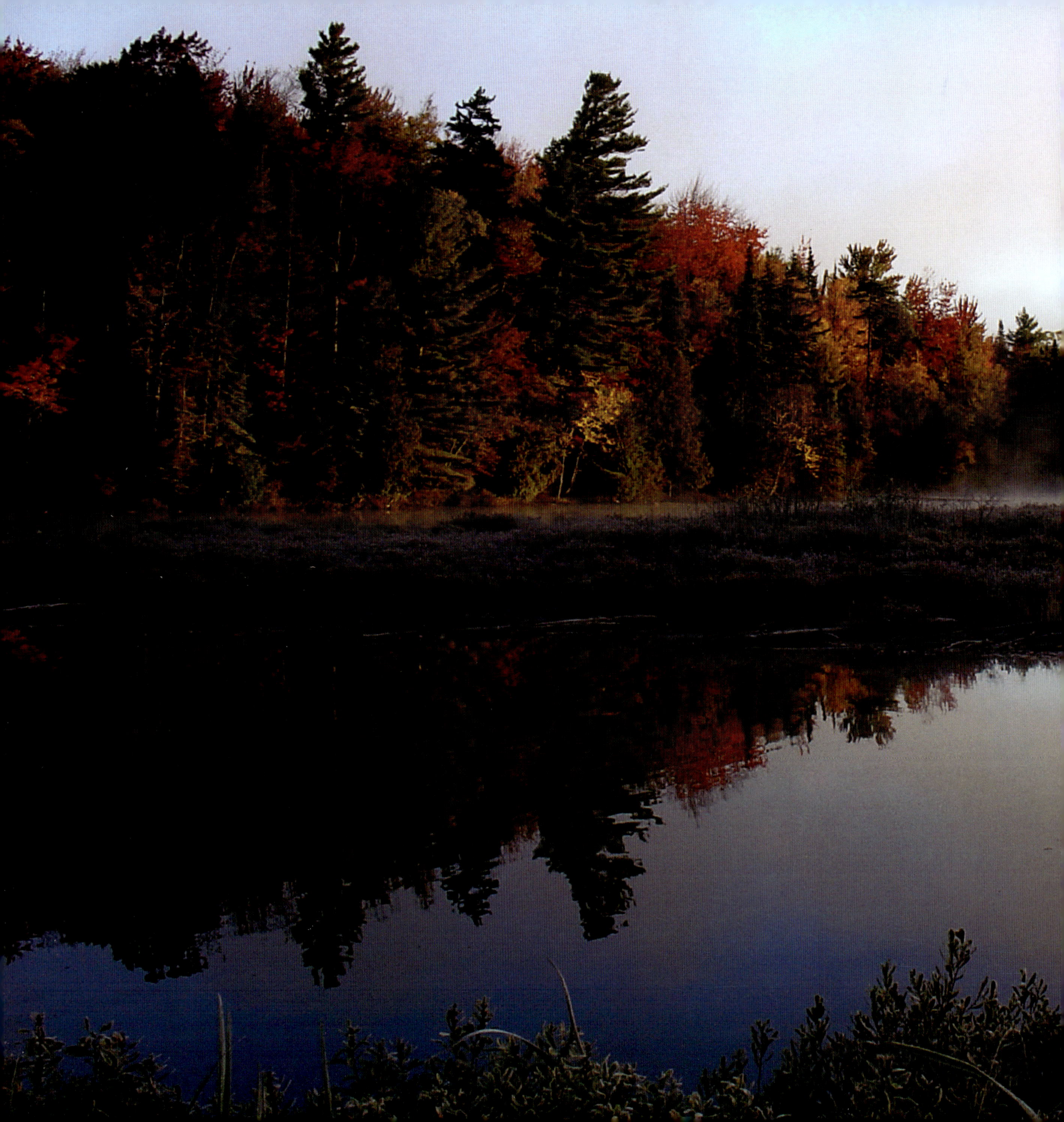

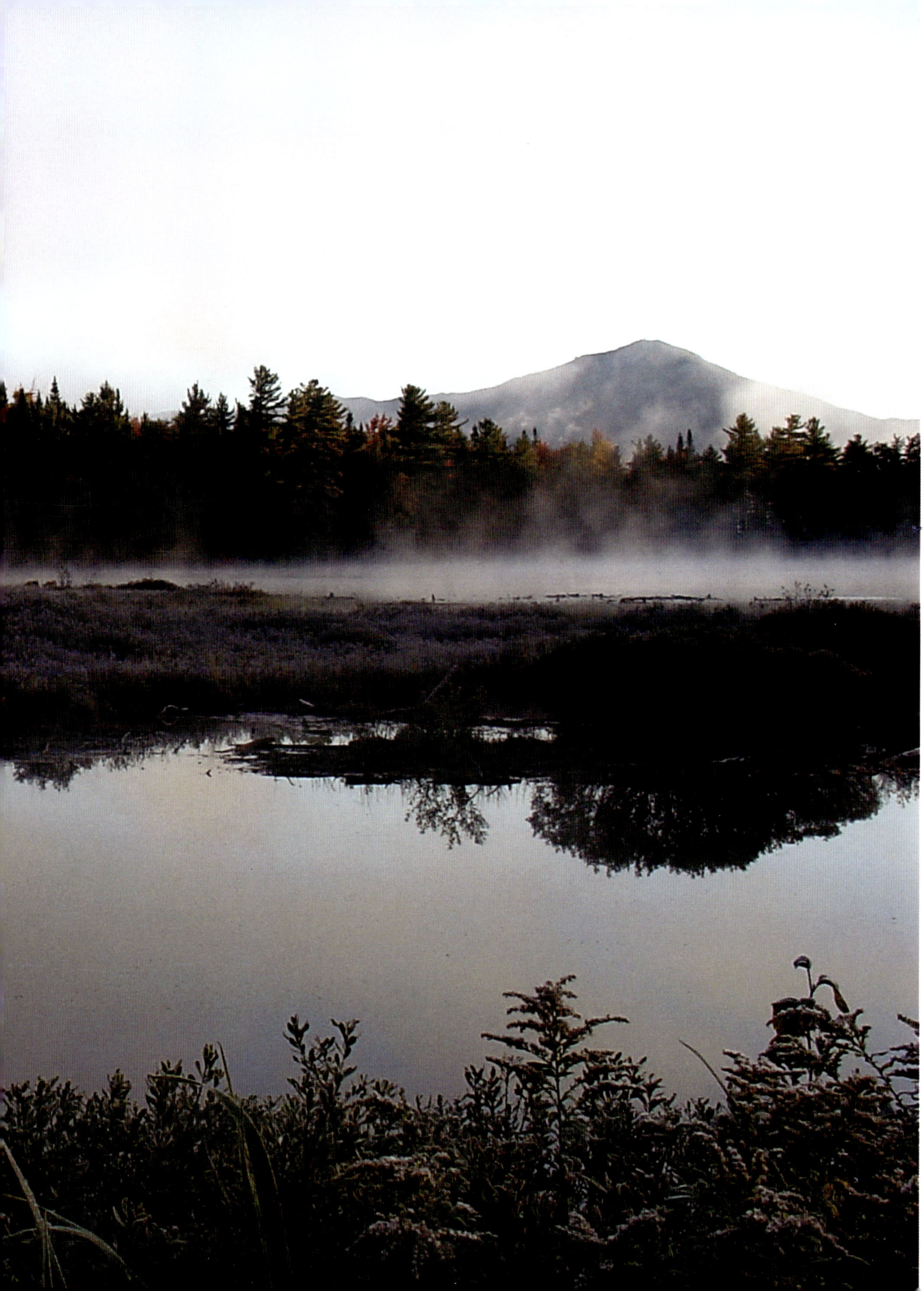

Still waters in the early morning give Lake Placid its name. The nearby village hosted the Winter Olympics in 1932 and 1980, and to this day its training center benefits thousands of Olympic hopefuls from around the world.

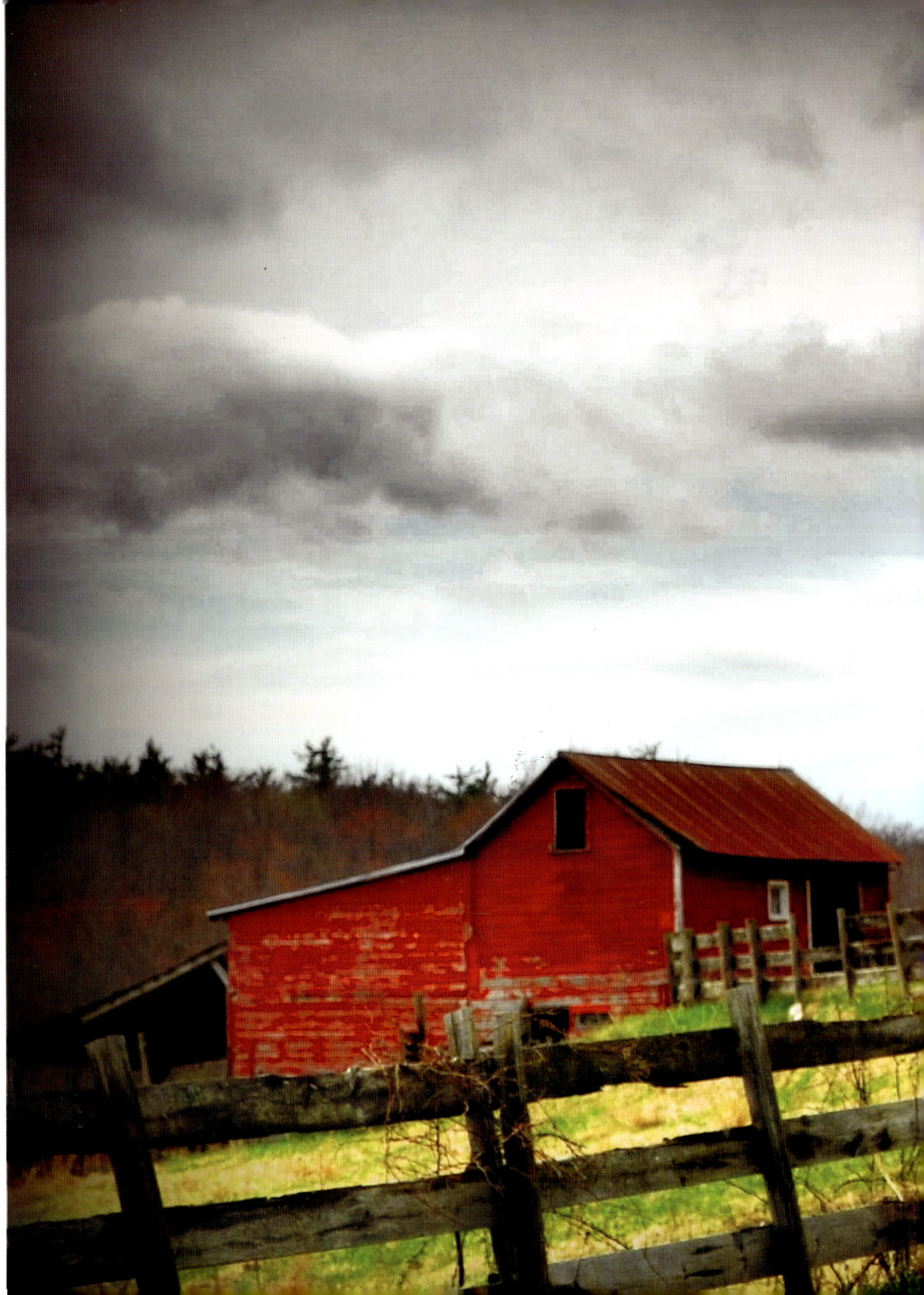

An iconic red-painted farm and silo sits near the upstate village of Ghent, just off the Taconic Parkway. Praised for its aesthetic integration into the landscape, the over 100-mile Taconic Parkway is the longest continuous parkway in New York.

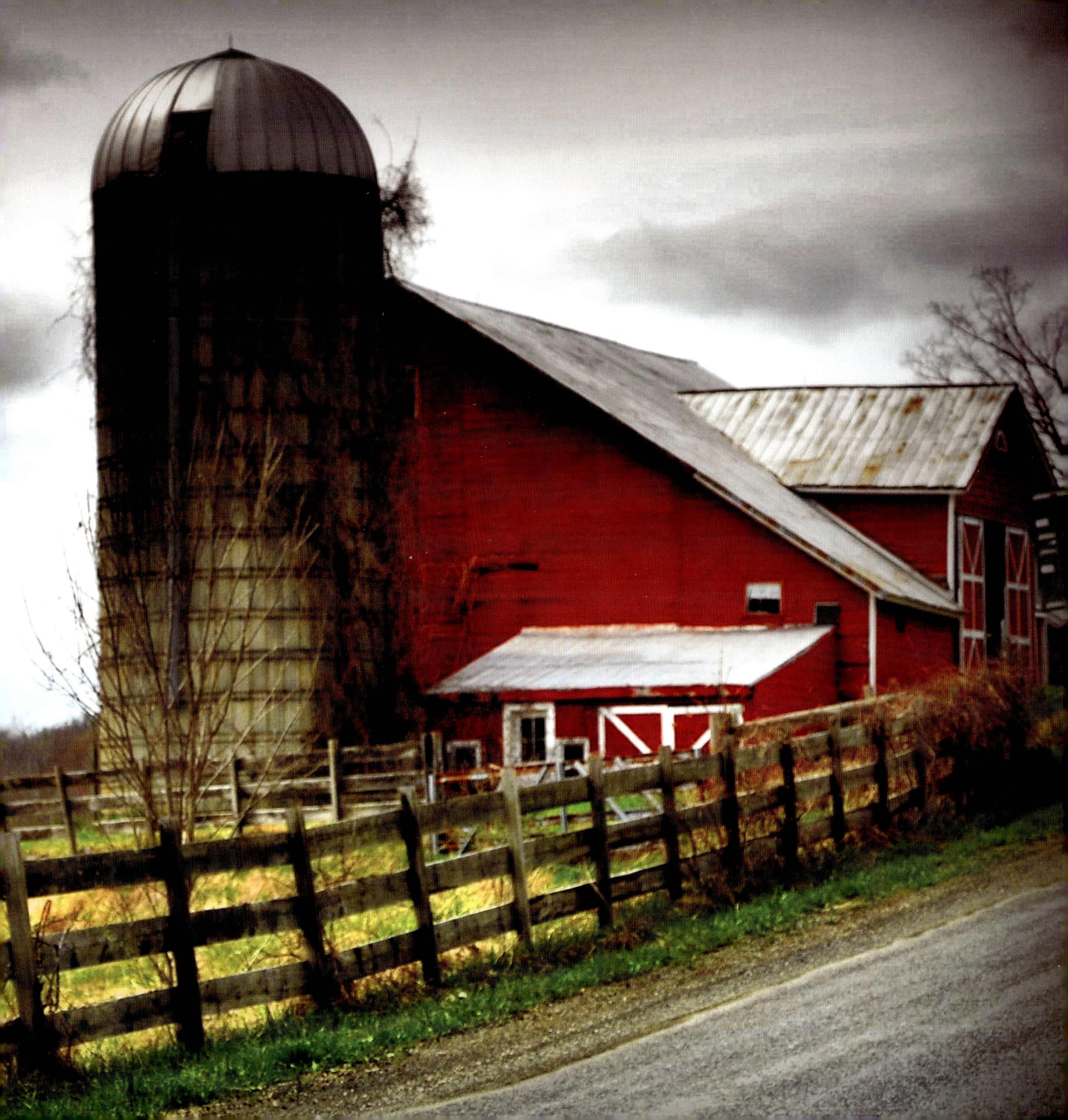

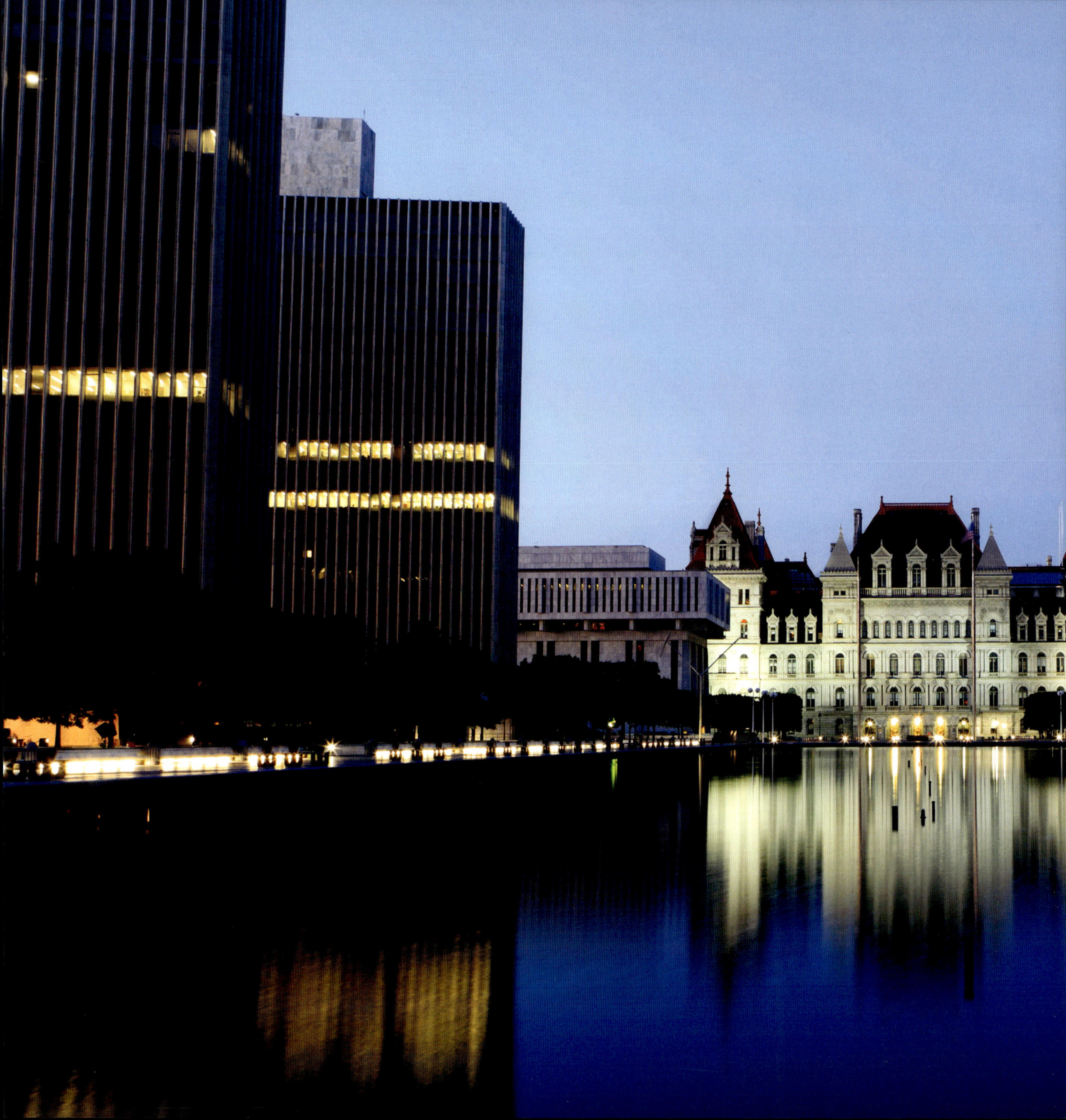

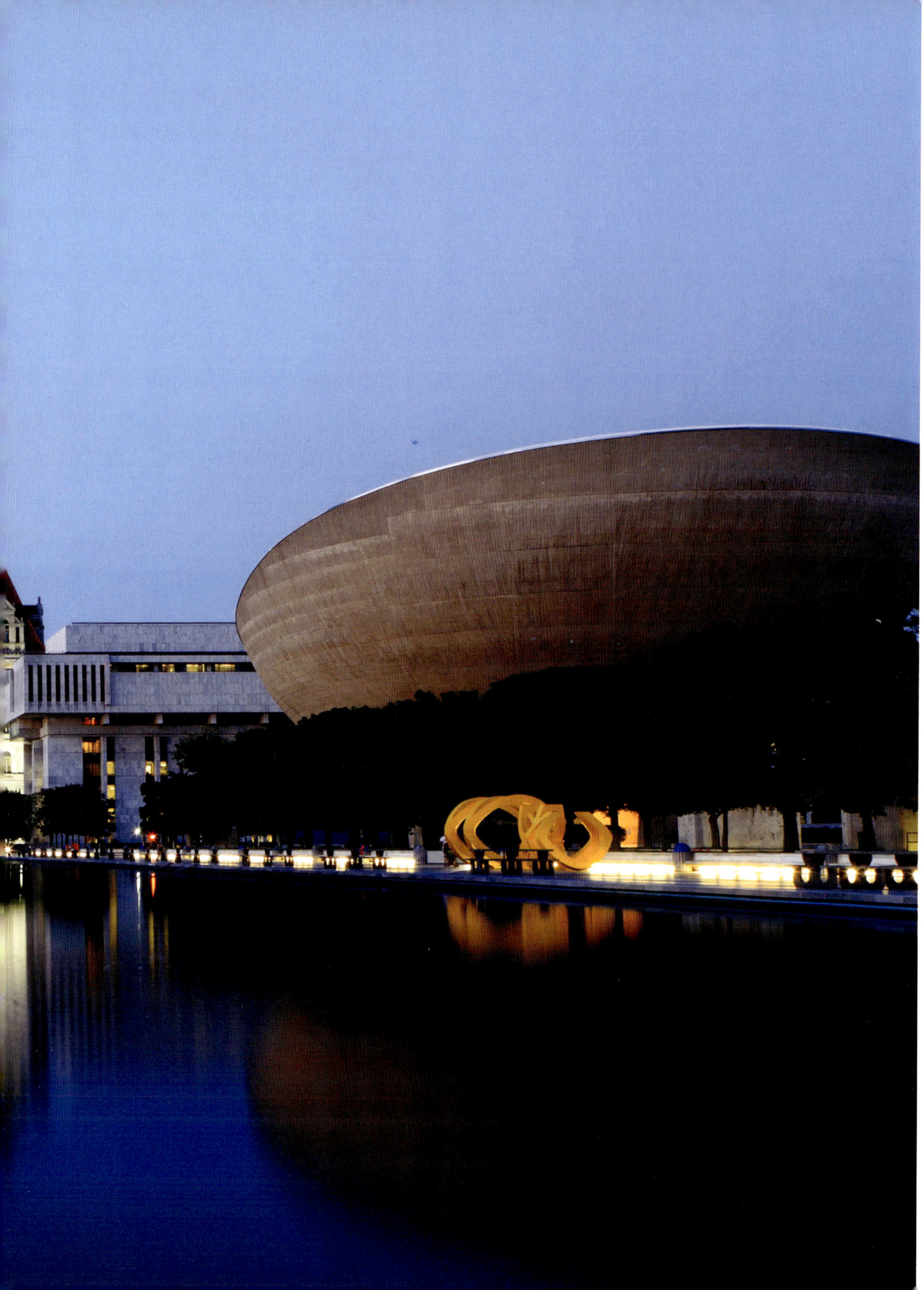

Albany's elaborate New York State Capitol Building, fashioned after Paris' Hotel de Ville, is nestled in the epicenter of Rockefeller Empire State Plaza, a complex also featuring state buildings, a skating rink, and a formidable collection of modern art.

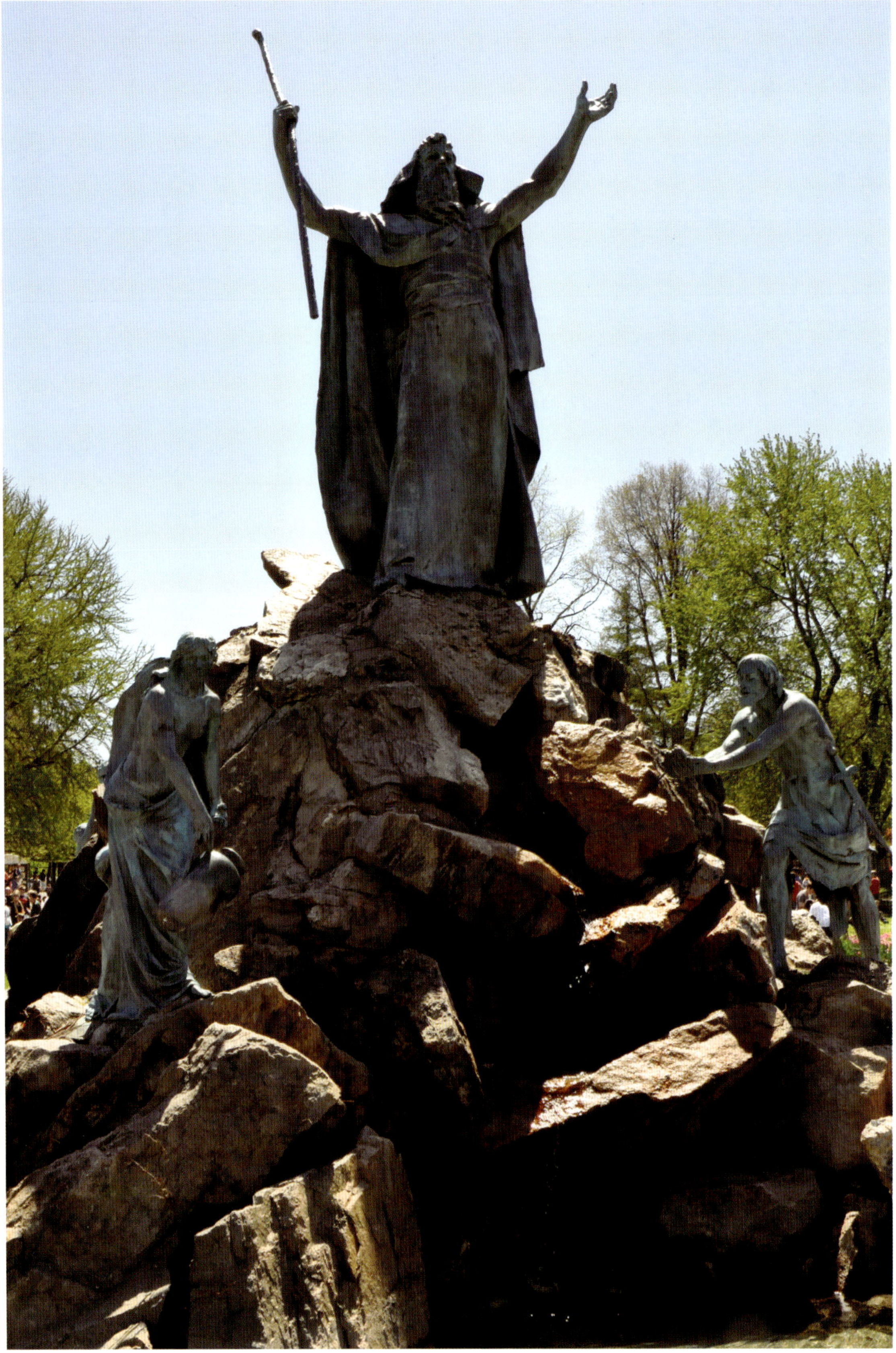

Perhaps the least-understood monument in Albany's Washington Park is Kings Fountain. Unveiled in 1893 and depicting Moses splitting the rock for water, it symbolizes local town patriarch Rufus King's skill in banking and mercantilism.

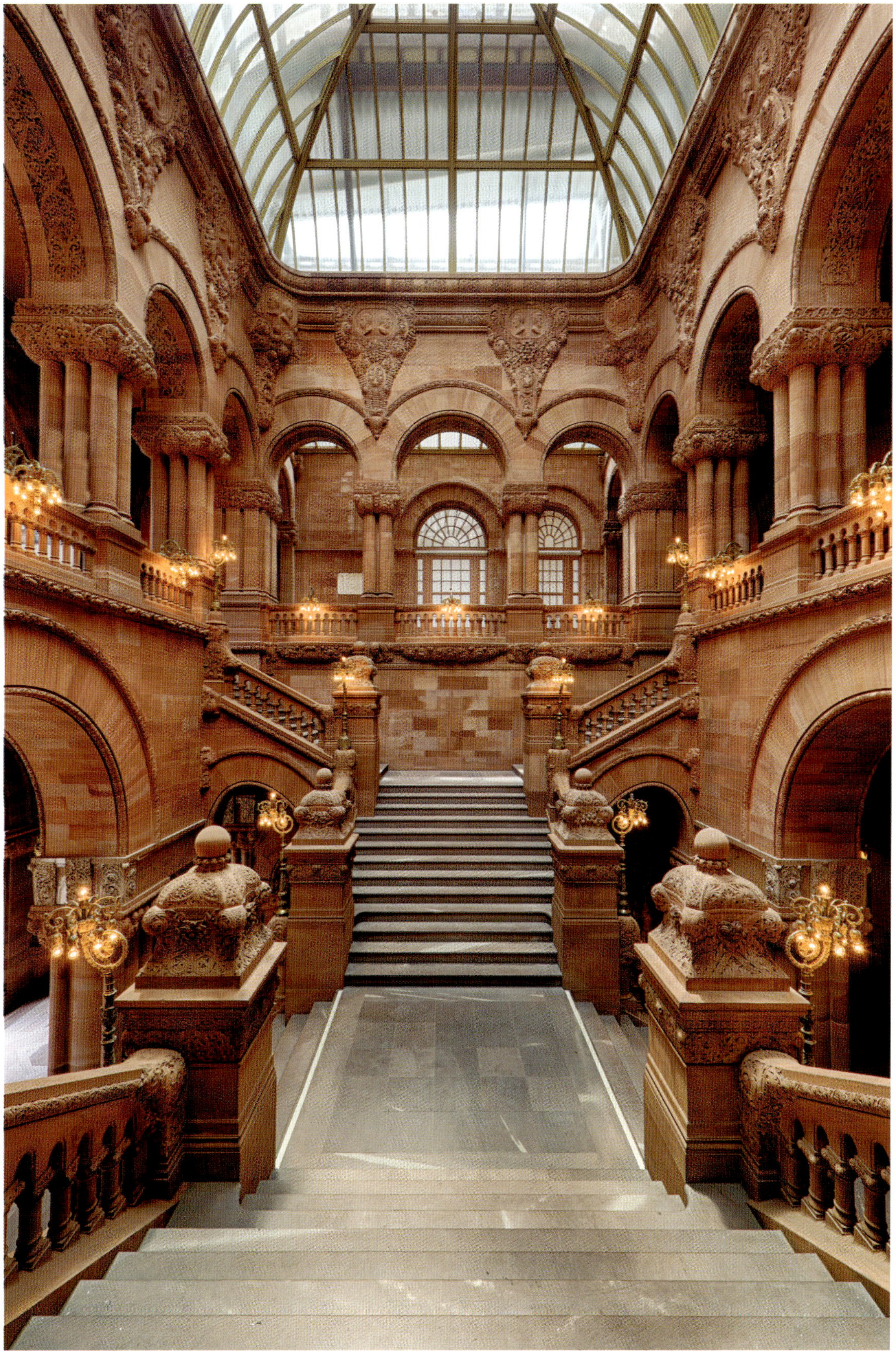

The New York State Capitol Building took 32 years and $25 million to build. Inside is the Great Staircase, which features more than 300 carvings of notable New Yorkers.

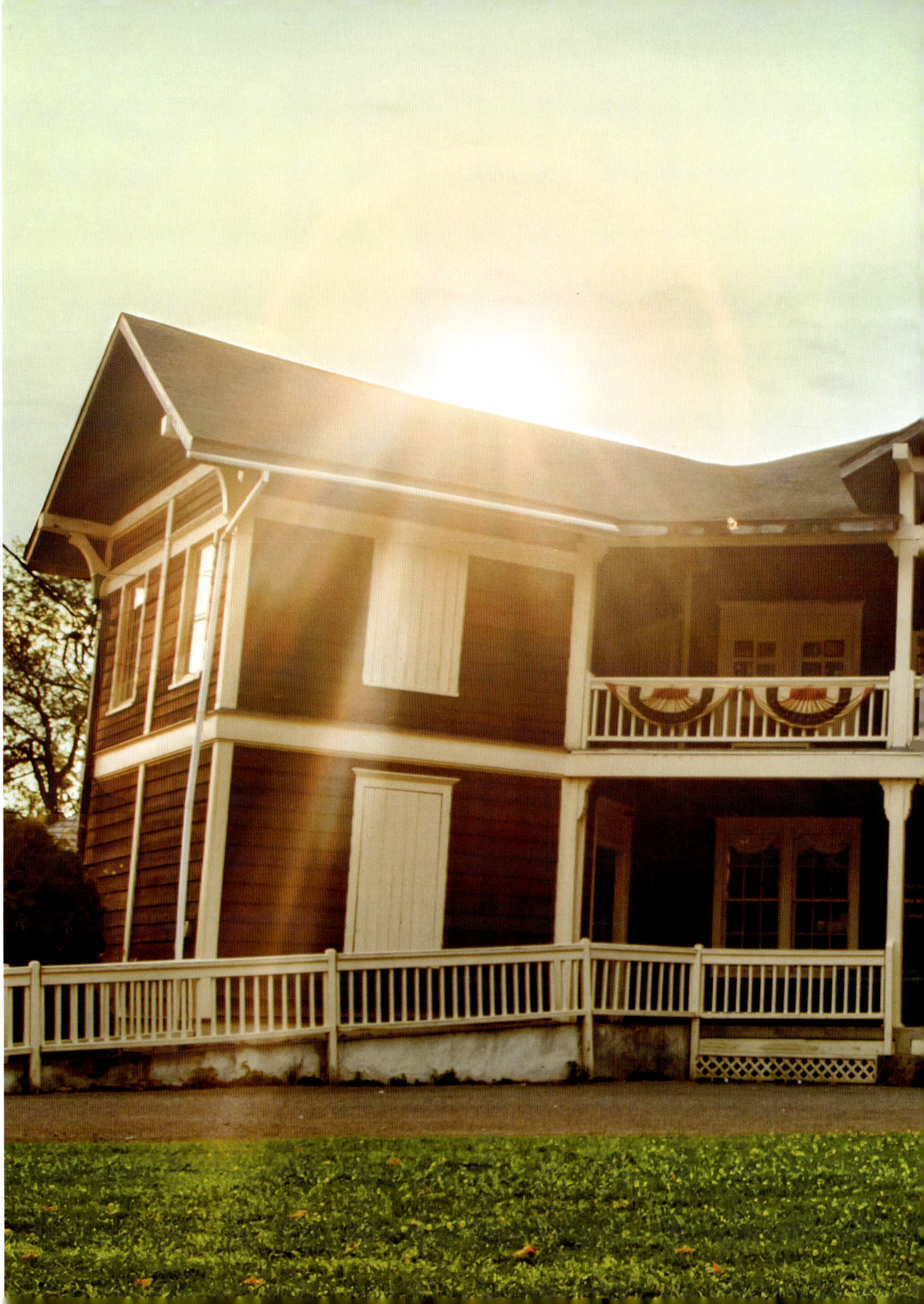

A charming, turn-of-the-century Pavillion rests in an idyllic country setting on Little York Lake, providing an unlikely home for one of the finest theaters in the central New York region, the Cortland Repertory Theatre.

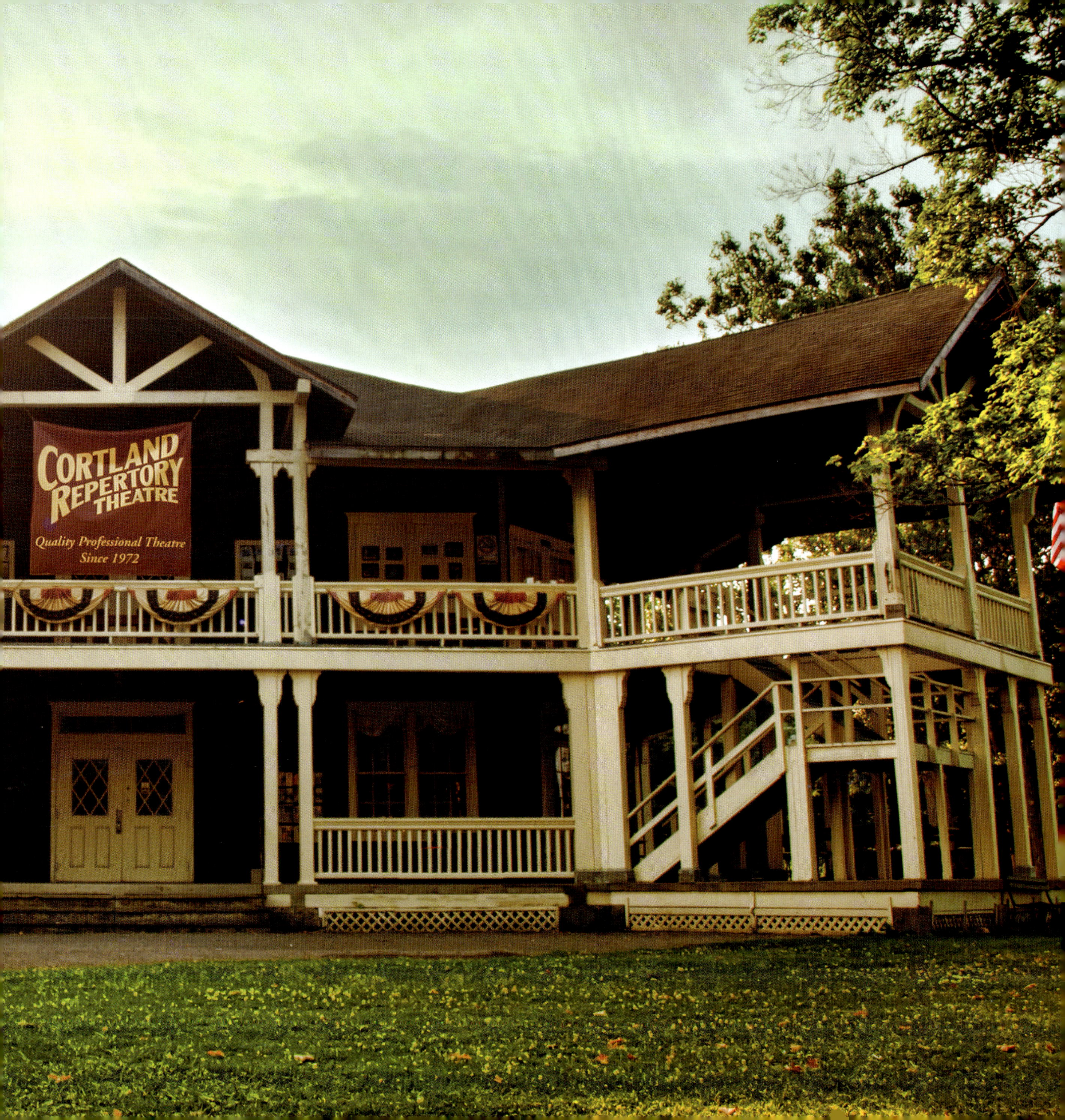
CORTLAND REPERTORY THEATRE
Quality Professional Theatre
Since 1972

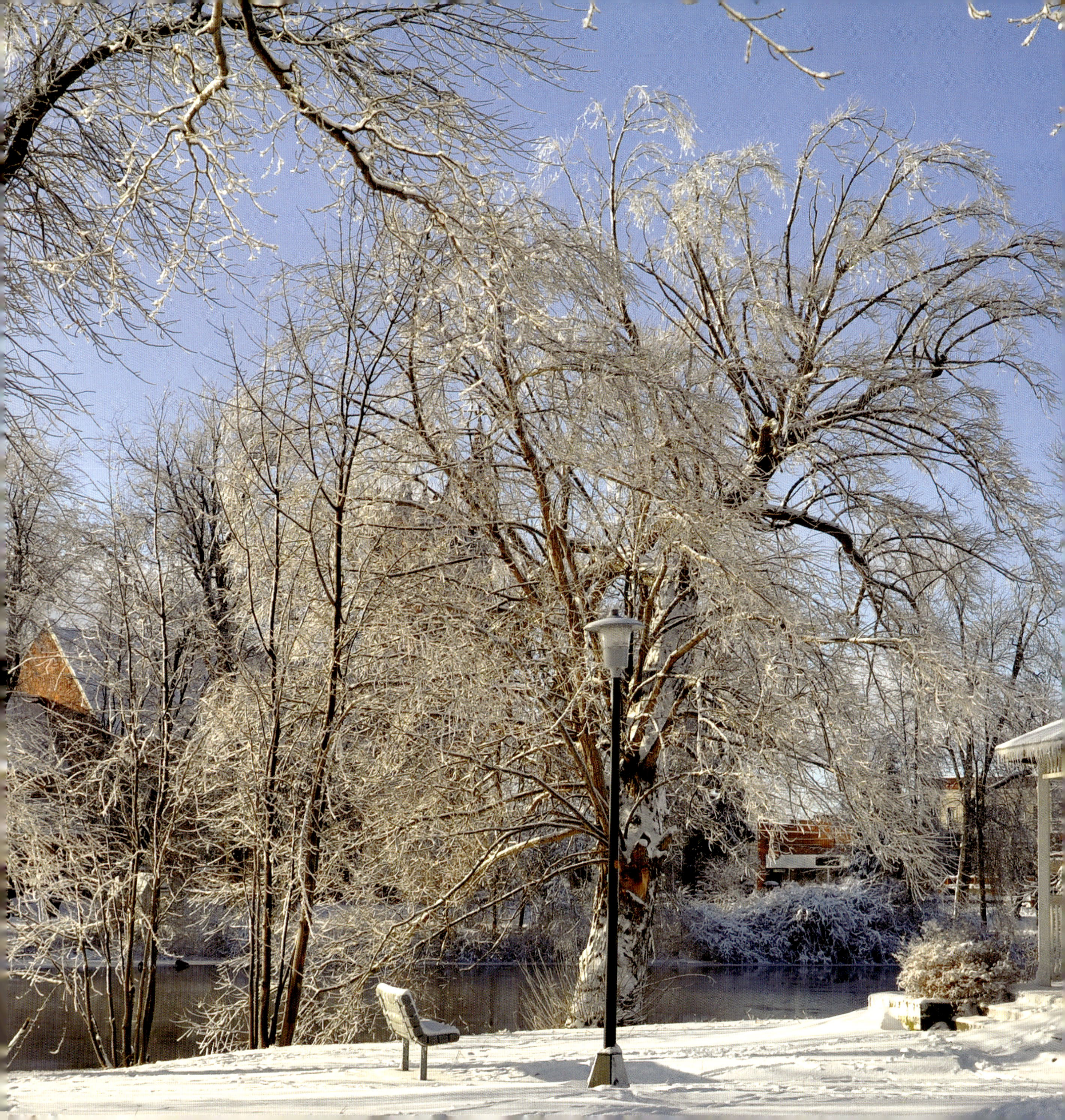

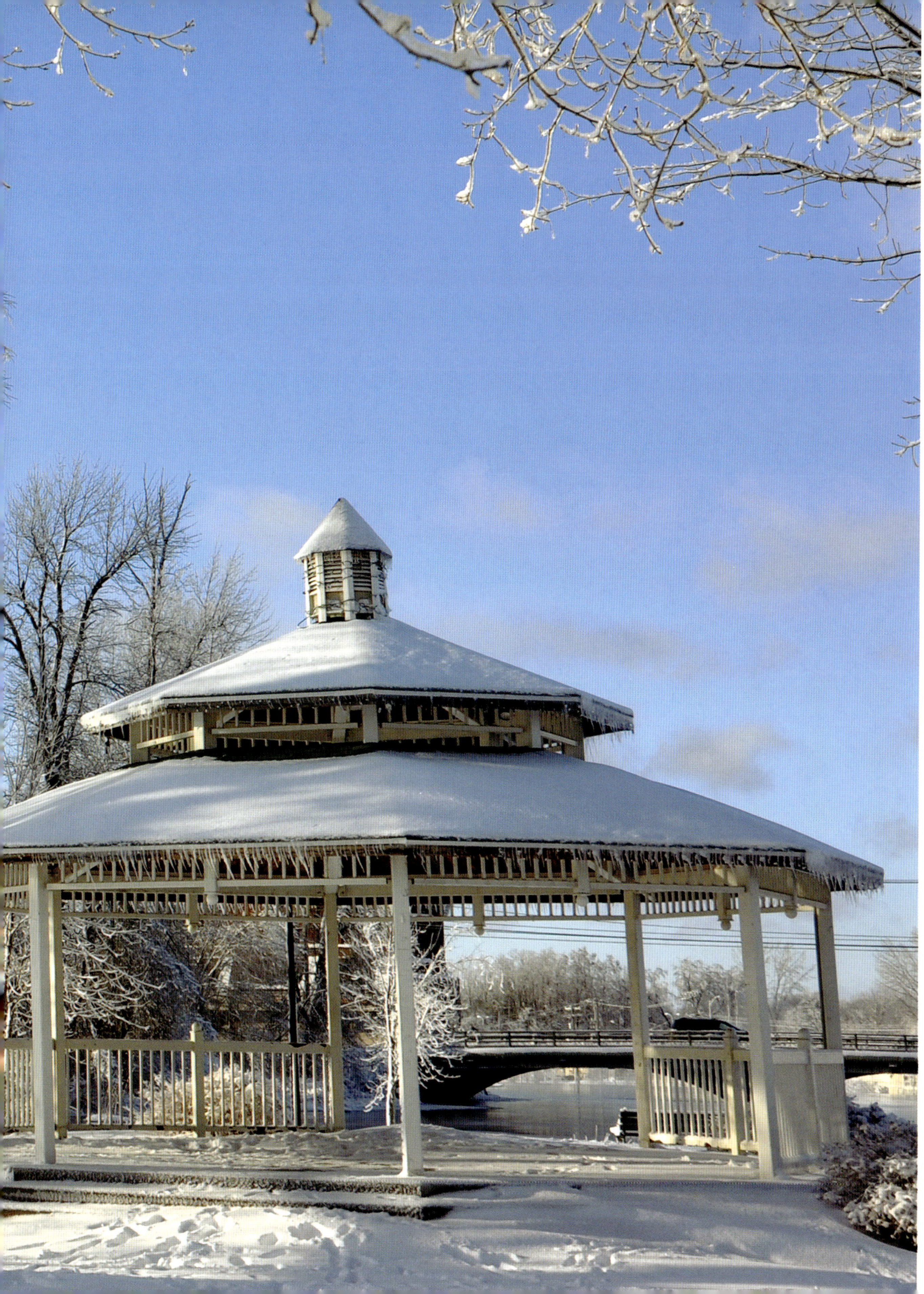

Winter snows coat the small town of Potsdam in northern New York. An educational hub, the town boasts the college of SUNY Potsdam and engineering school Clarkson University, as well as nearby St. Lawrence University and SUNY Canton.

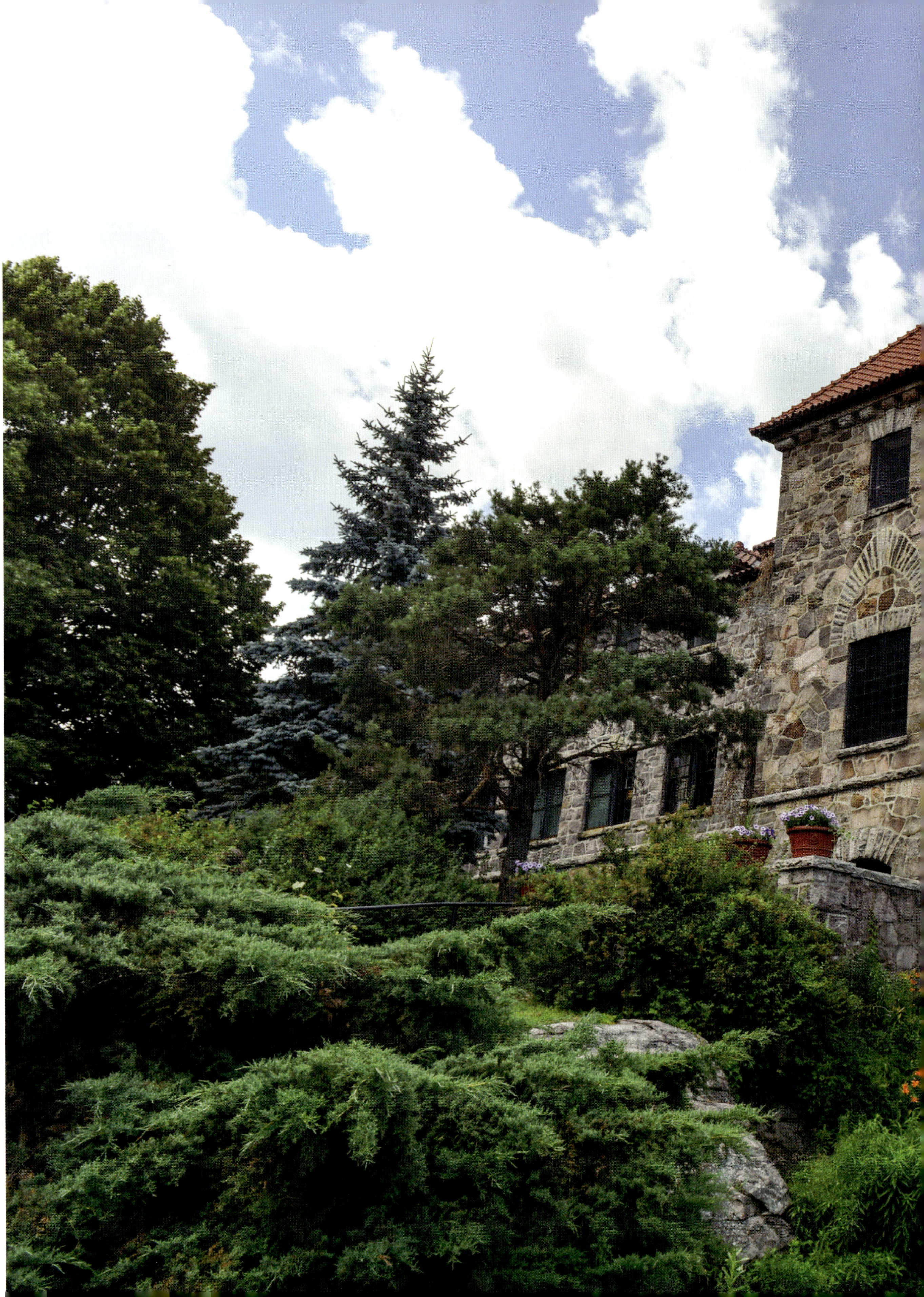

Its turrets rising above Dark Island on the St. Lawrence Seaway, Singer Castle is known for its narrow labyrinthine tunnels, hidden entrances, and secret passageways built for spying.

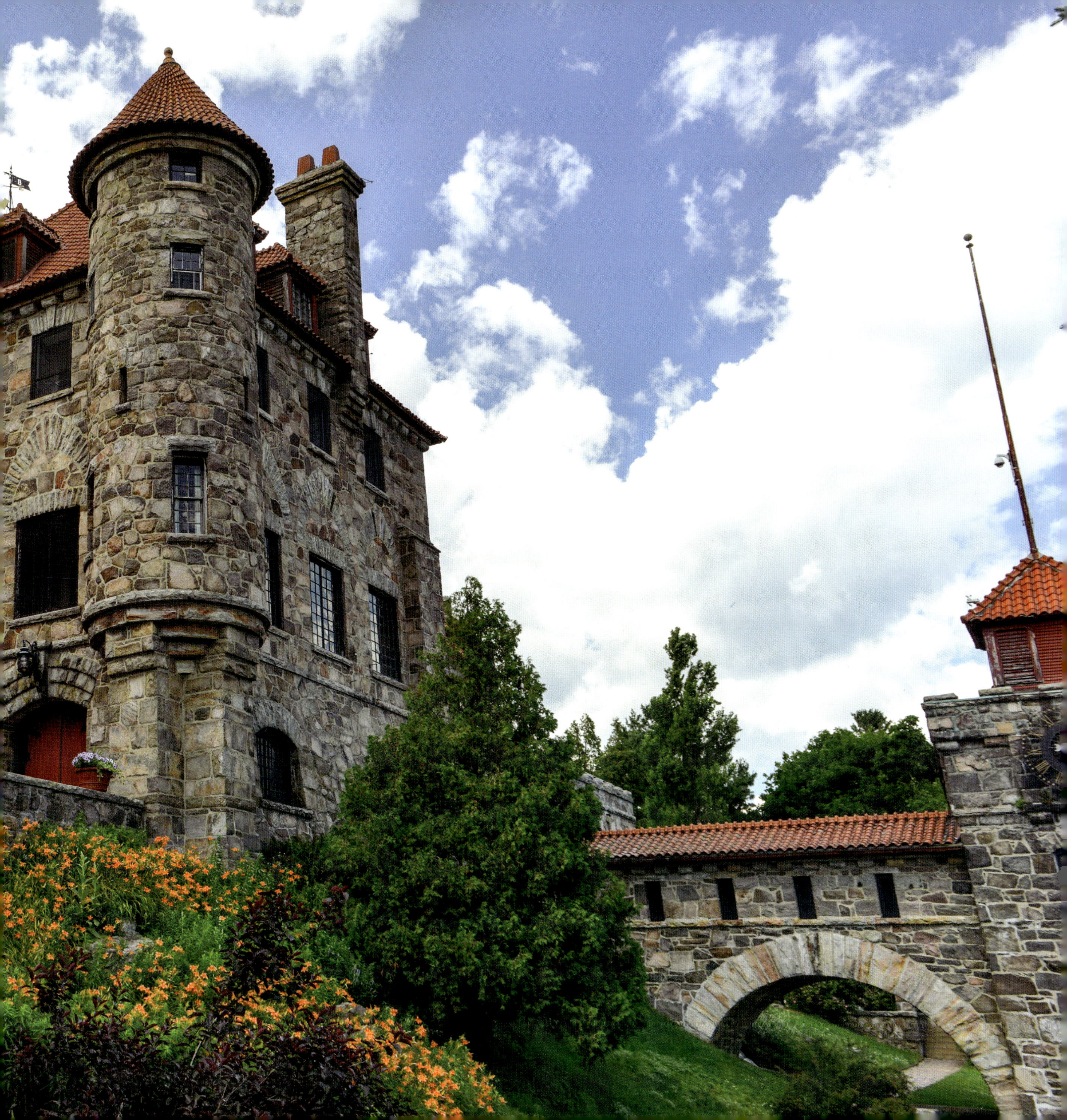

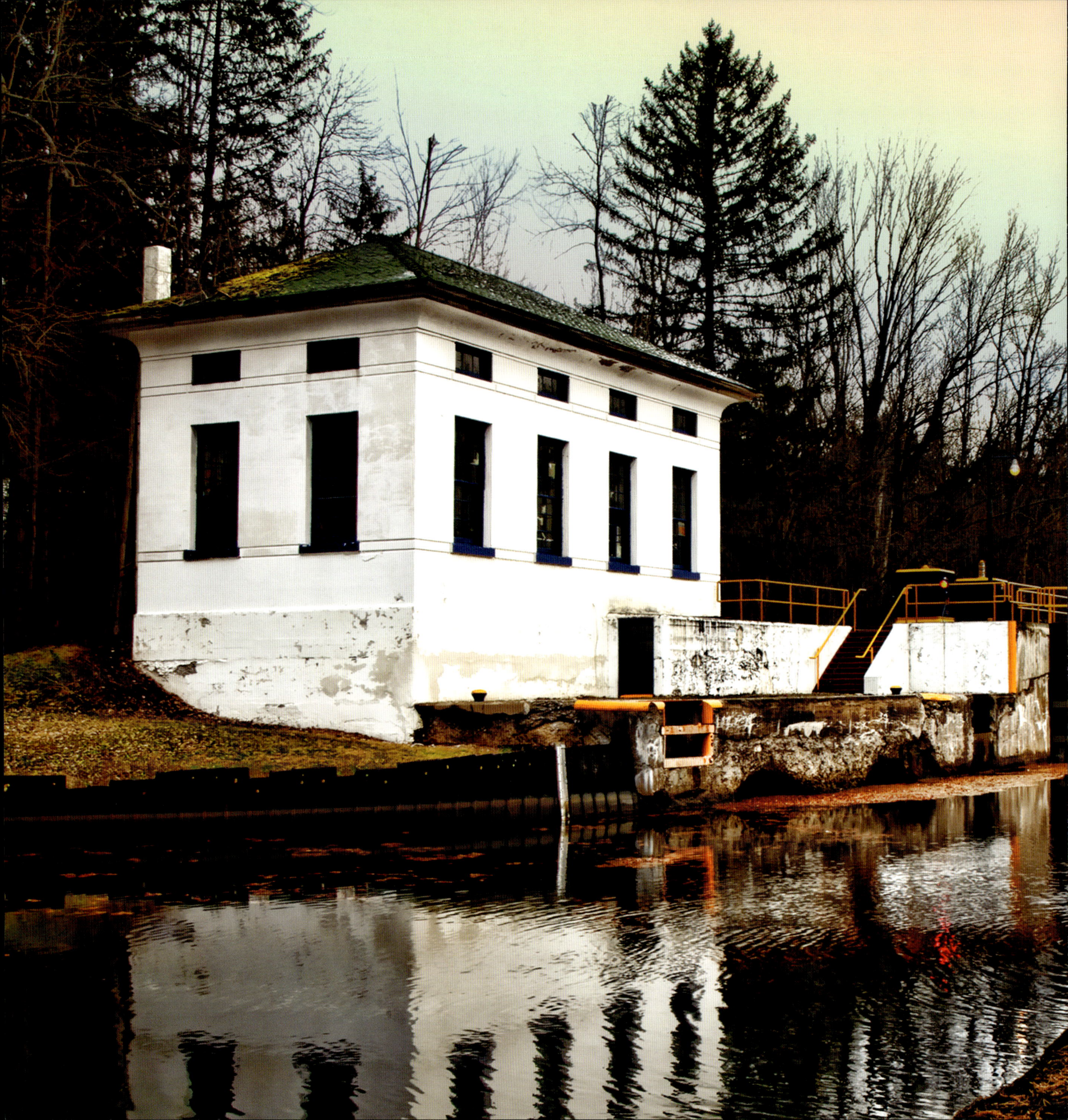

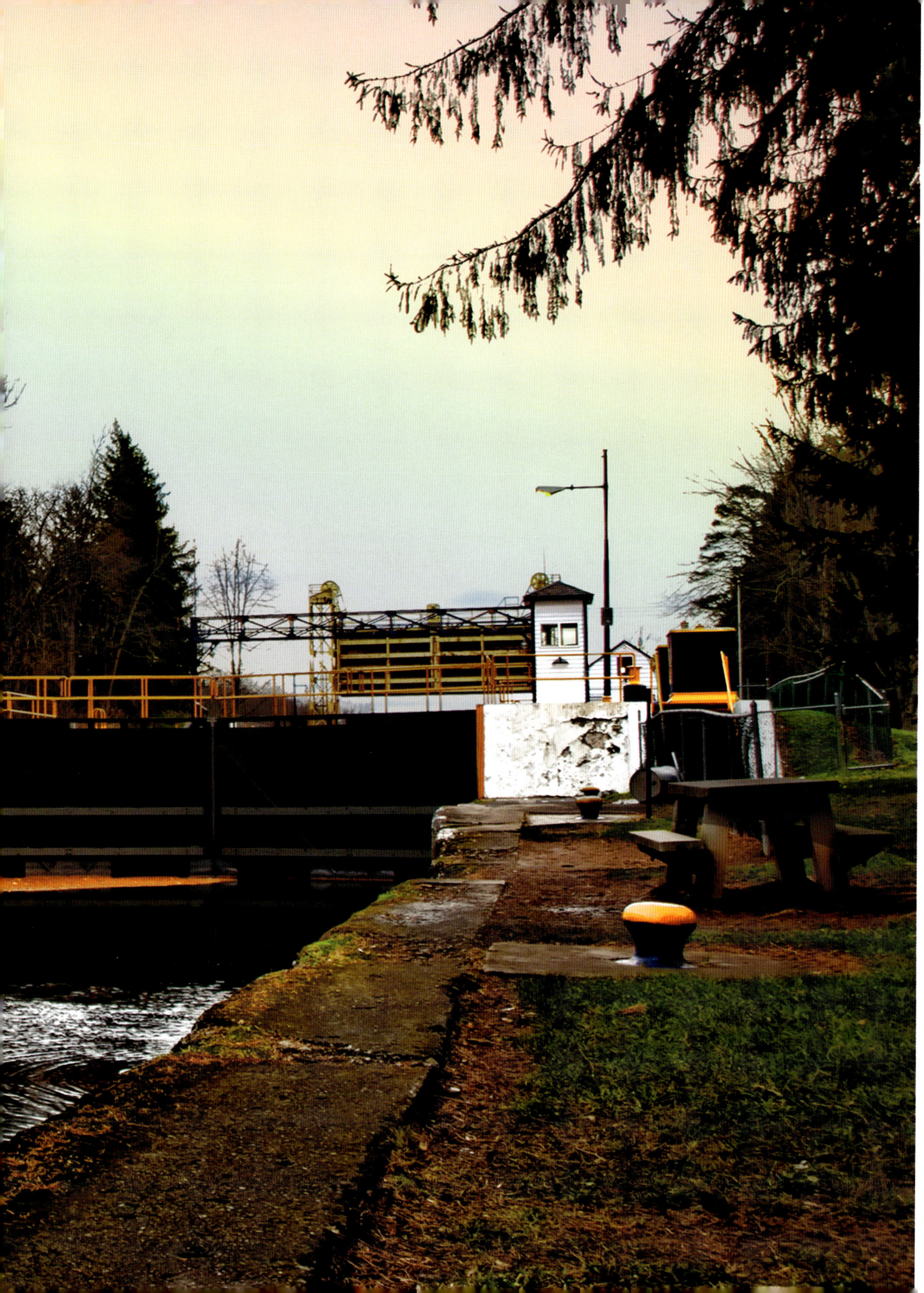

Linking Lake Erie to the Hudson River, the Erie Canal opened up western New York to the rest of the country in the early 1800s, creating a massive industrial and population boom.

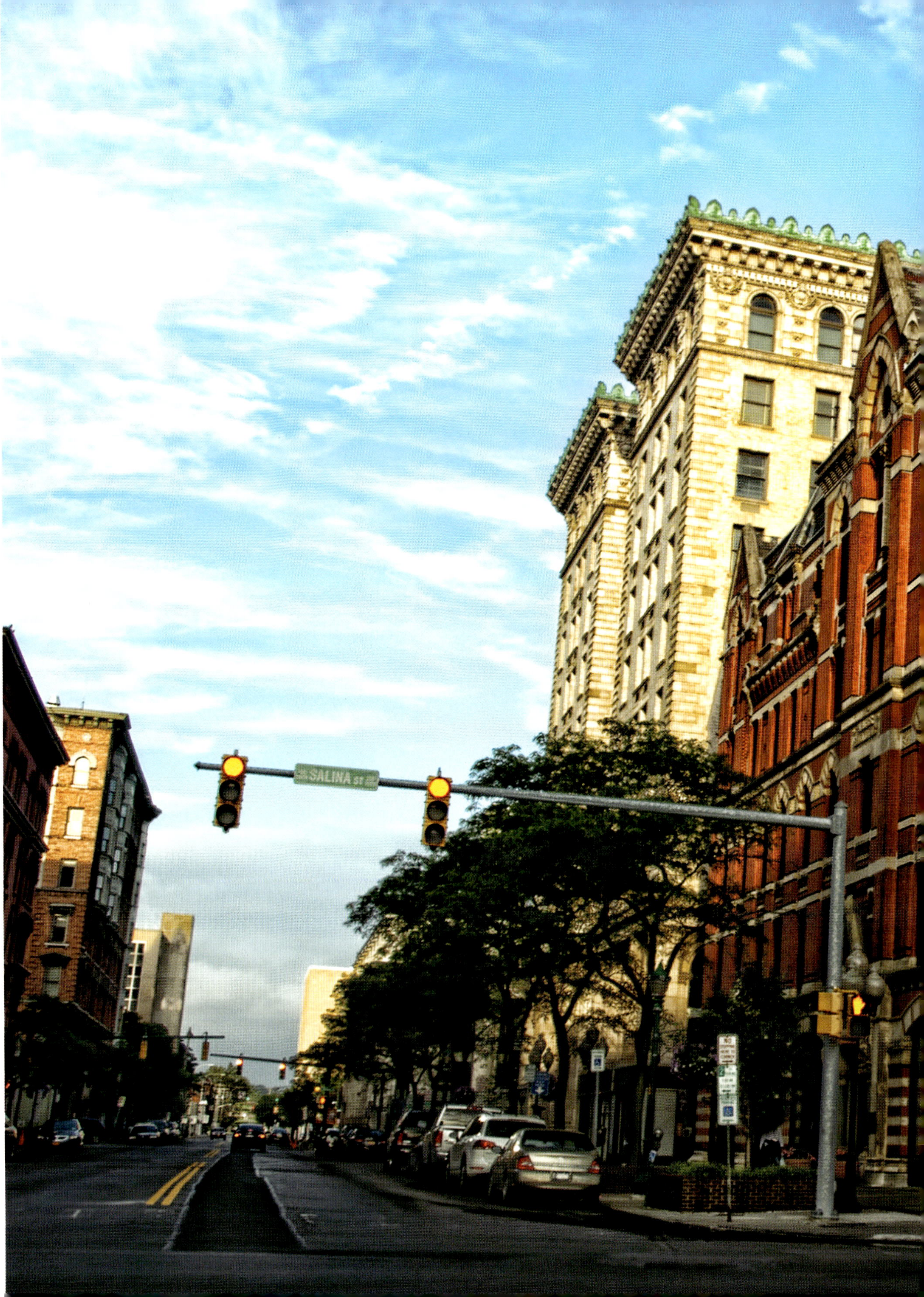

Within 20 miles of the beautiful Finger Lakes region lies New York's fifth most populous city, Syracuse. Here, the White Memorial Building exemplifies the textbook High Victorian Gothic work by architect Joseph Lyman Silsbee, typical of many of the buildings in the downtown Syracuse area.

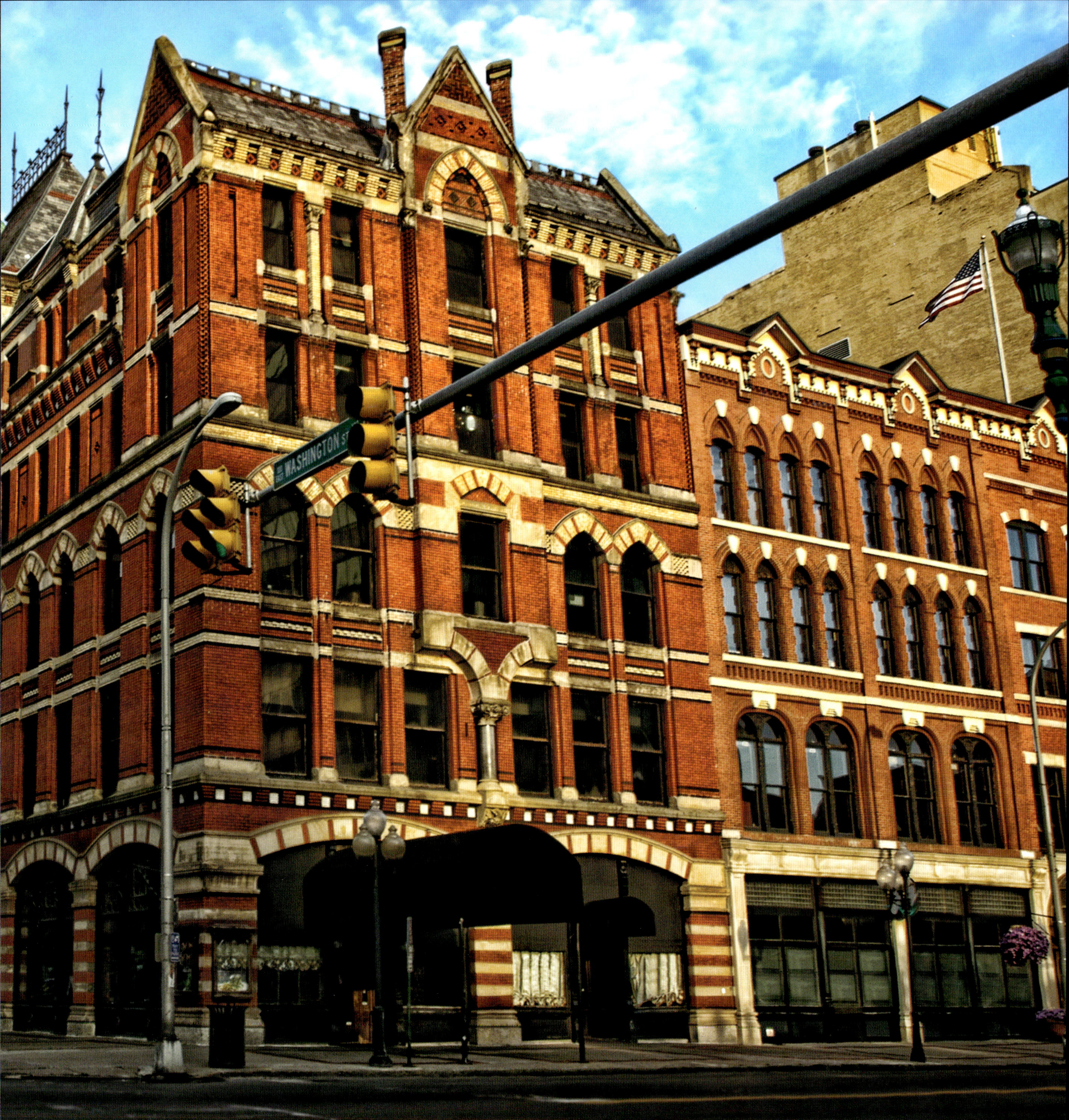
WASHINGTON ST

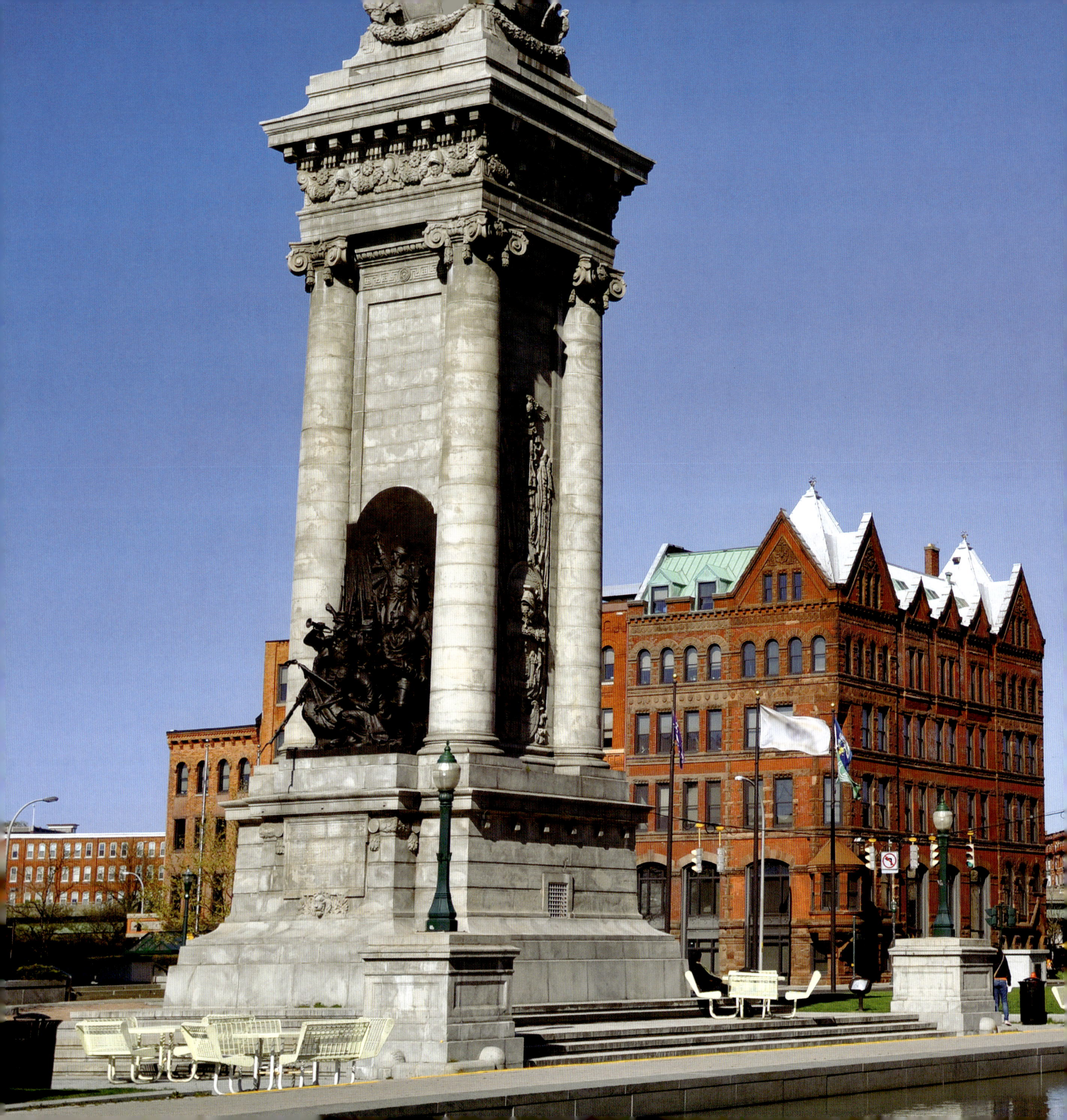

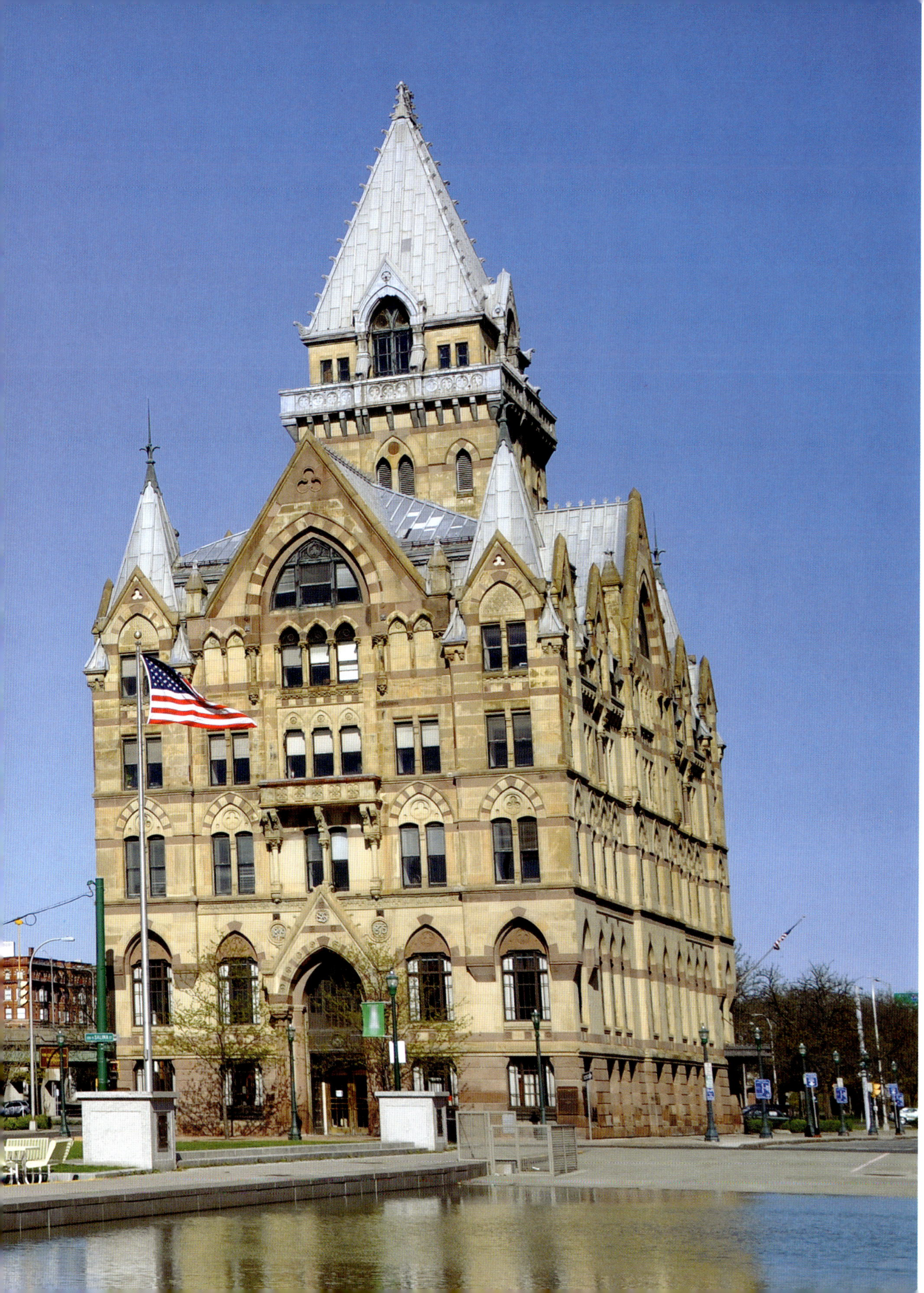

Adjacent to the Erie Canal lies Clinton Square and the old Syracuse Savings Bank Building. Its passenger elevator, the first in Syracuse in 1876, was a curiosity that drew visitors.

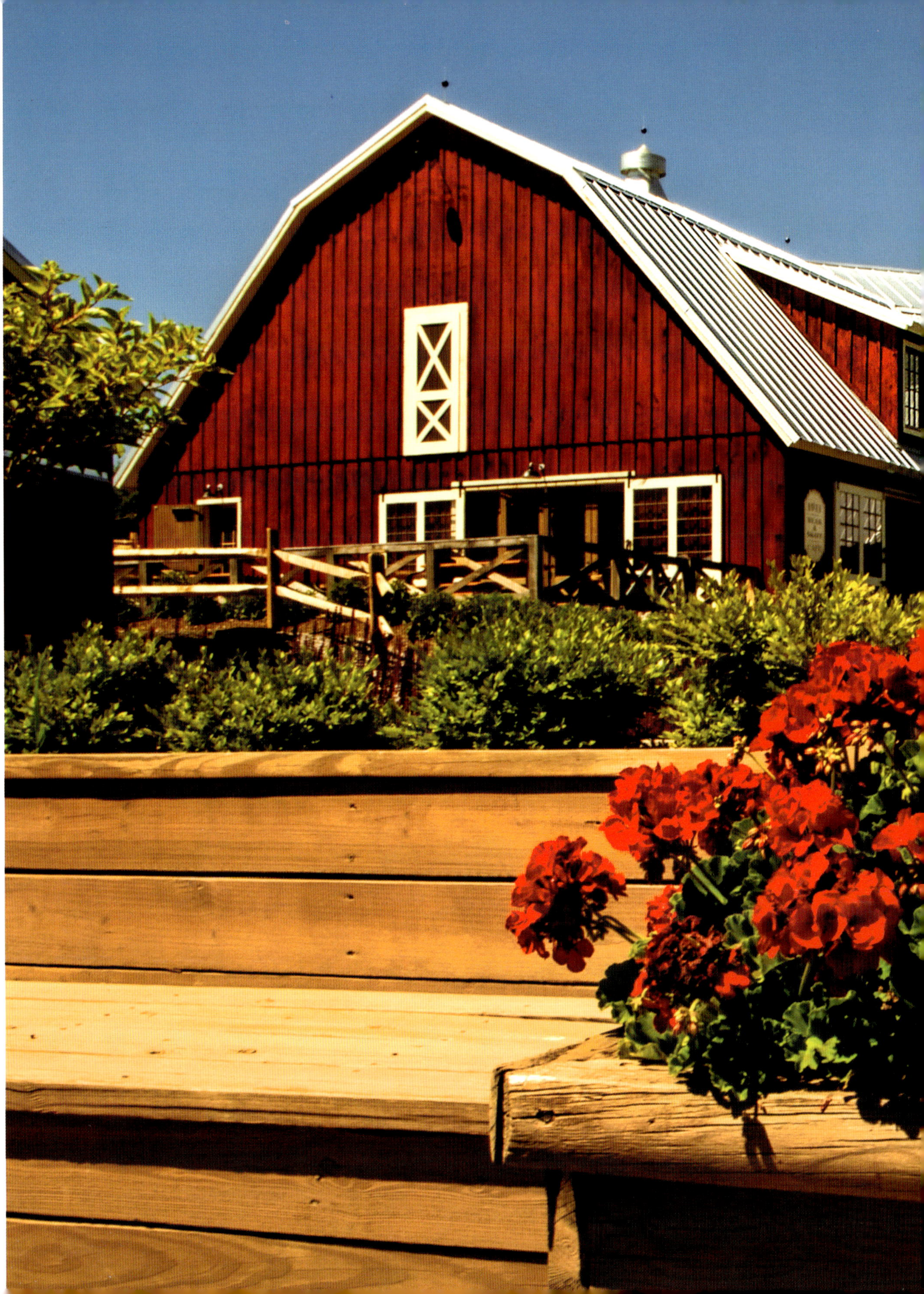

Growing and marketing more commercial varieties of fresh-market apples than any other region in the country, New York State averages 29.5 million bushels of production annually. Here, the homey and welcoming feel of the Beak and Skiff Apple Farms in Lafayette represent the state's nearly 700 apple growers.

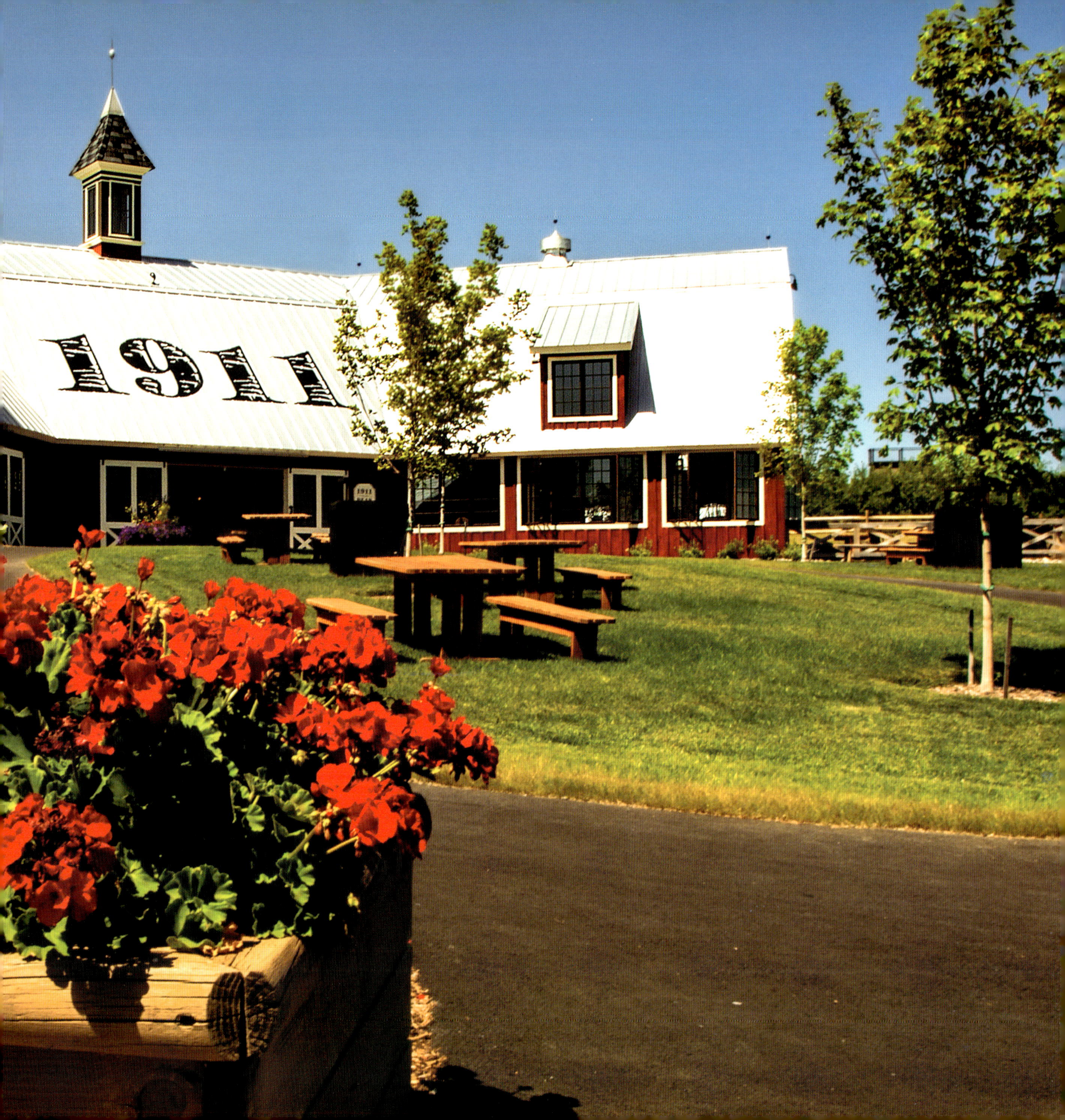
1911

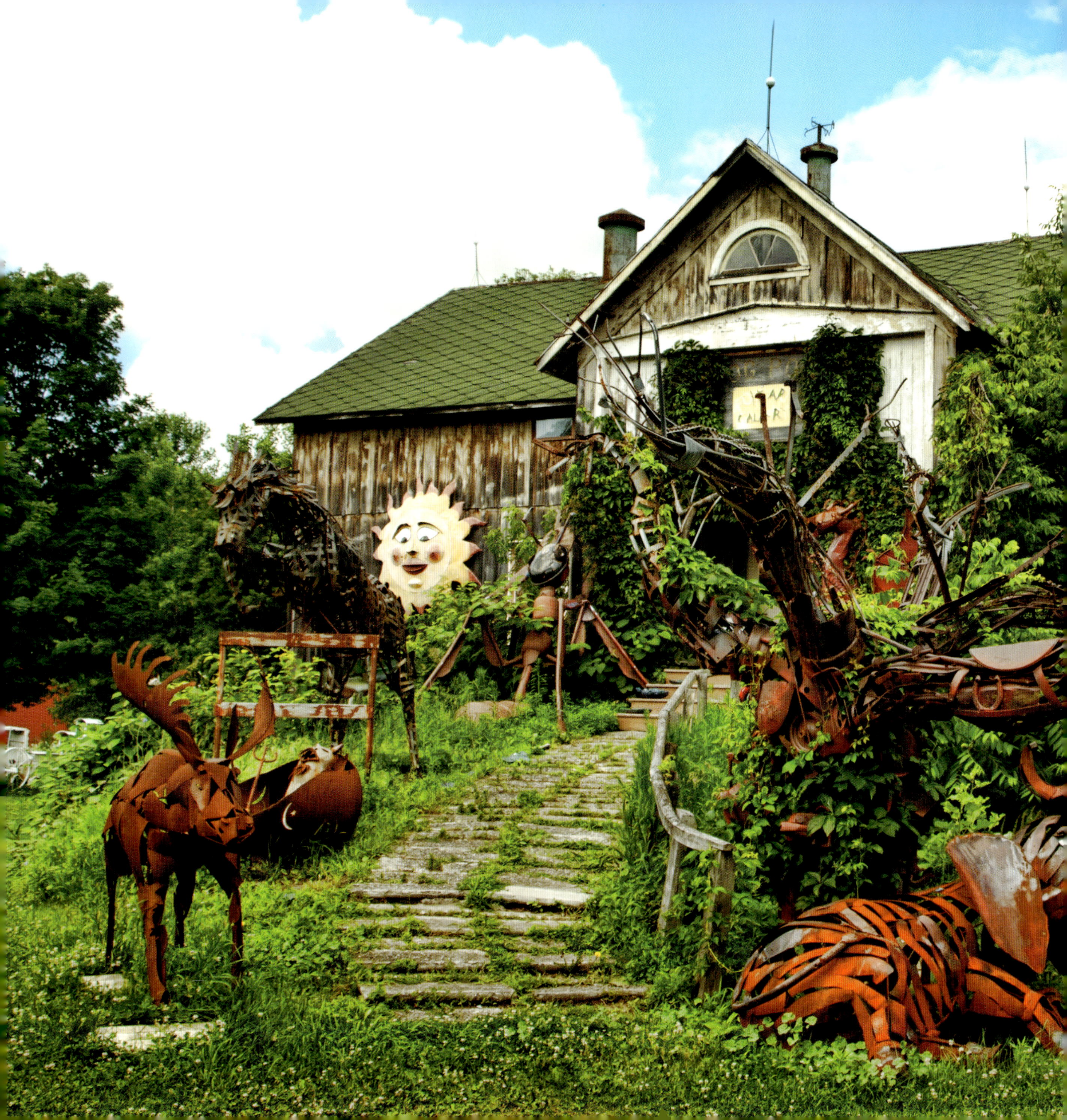

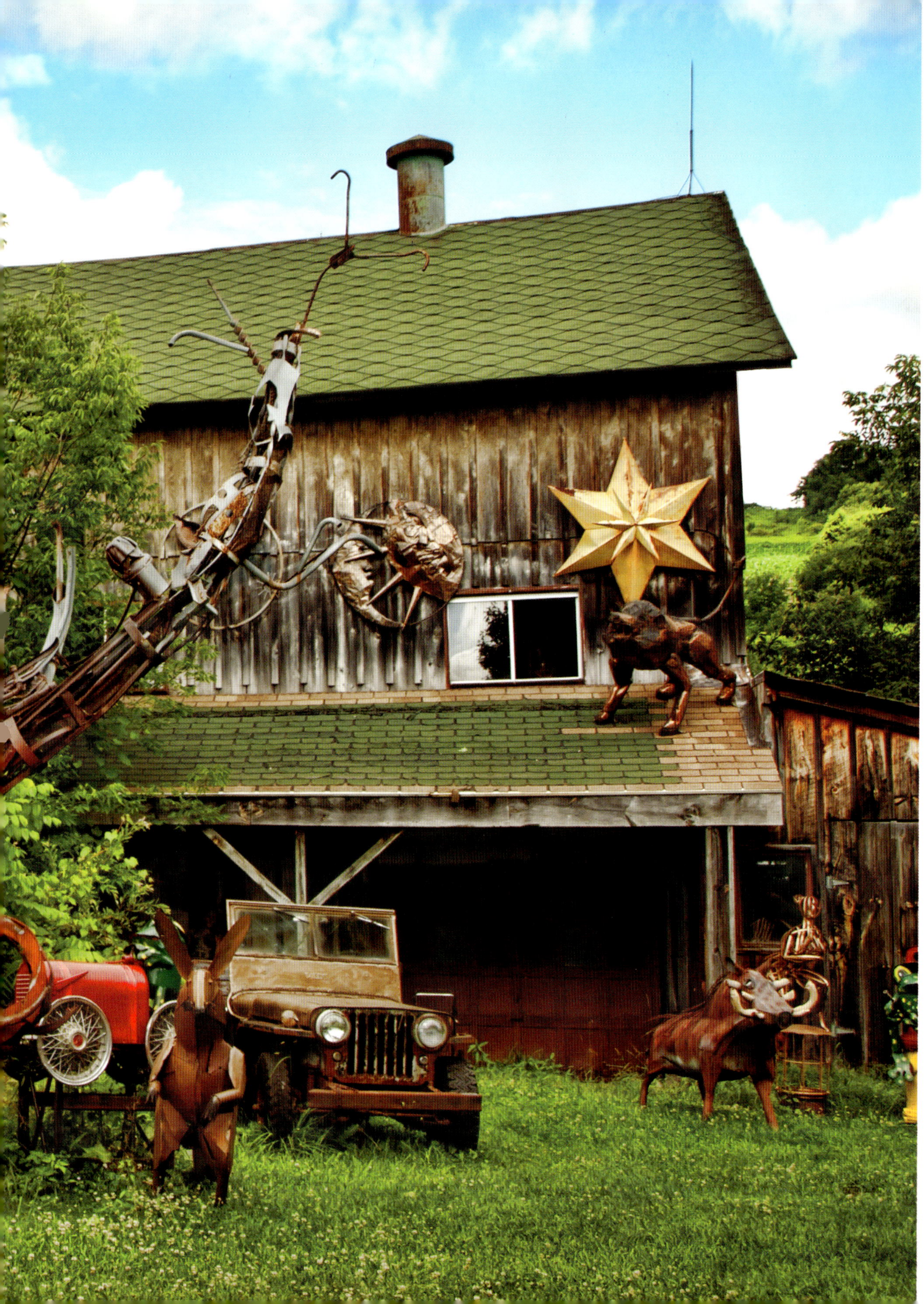

Intricate sculptures, monstrous animals, and whimsical creatures crafted from pre-used metal and wood greet visitors at the Frog Pond Farm Folk Art Gallery in Homer.

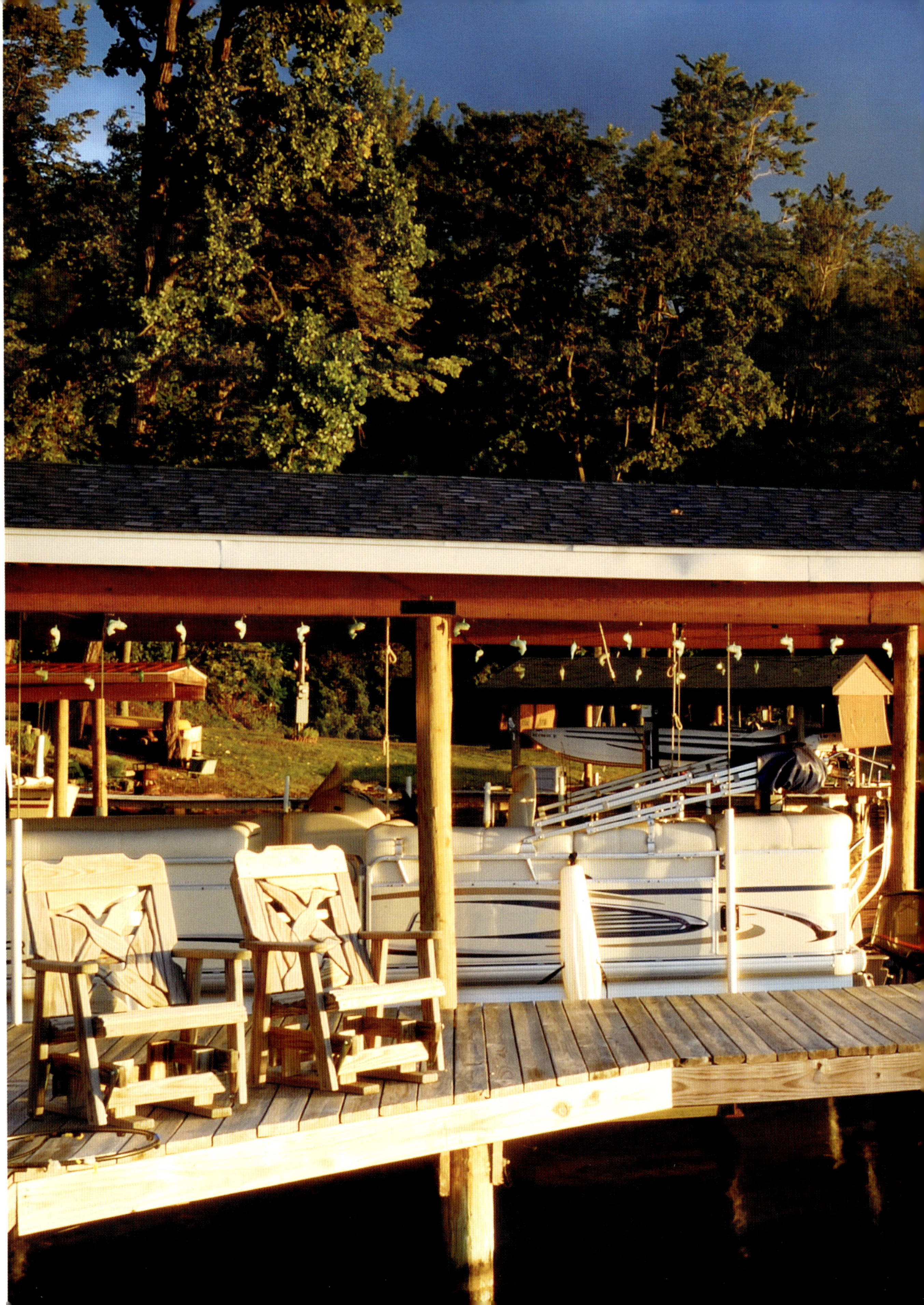

A lake house and pier peek out over a sunrise. Named after its narrow lakes formed by glaciers, the Finger Lakes region contains some of the state's most breathtaking scenery.

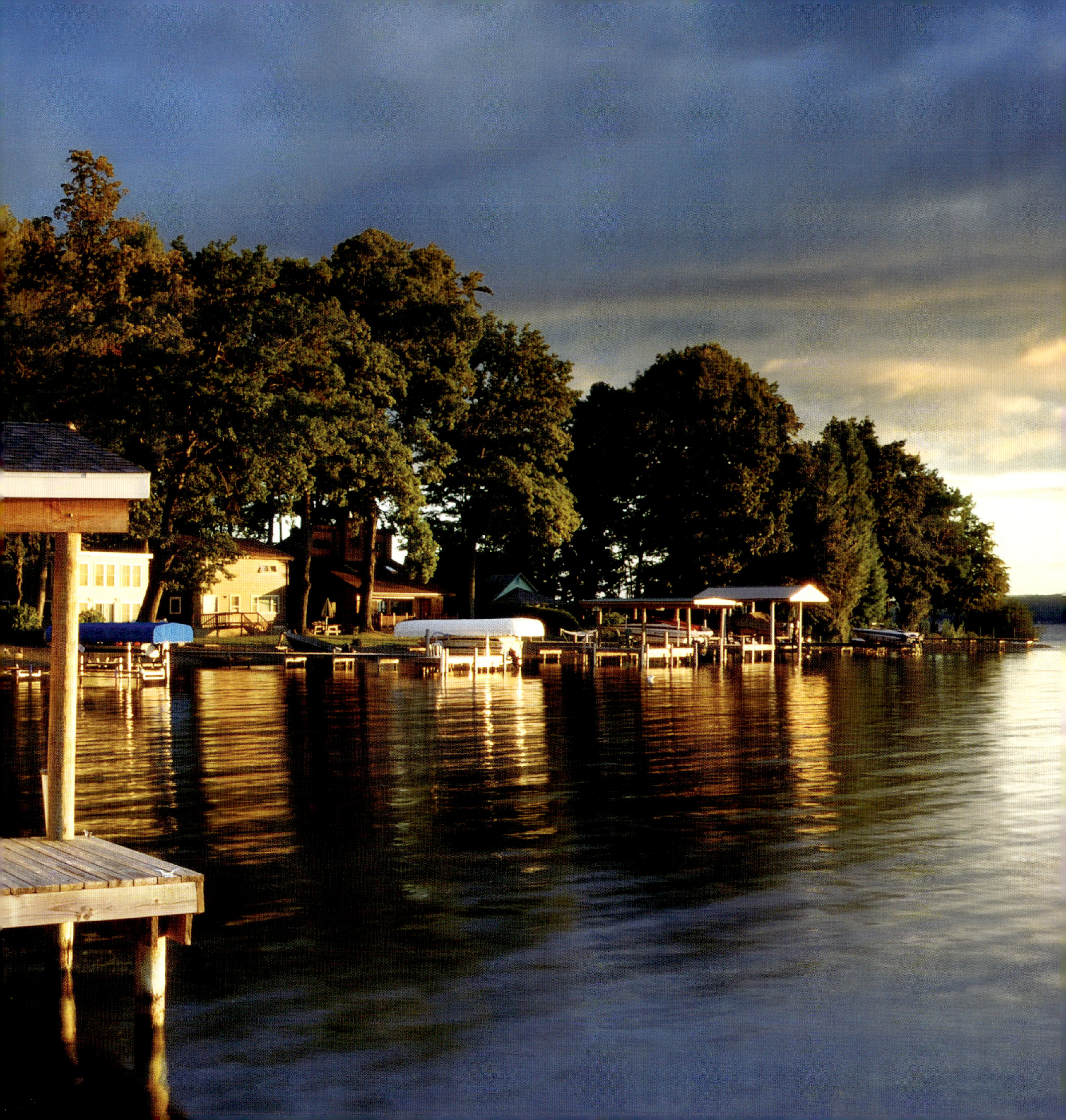

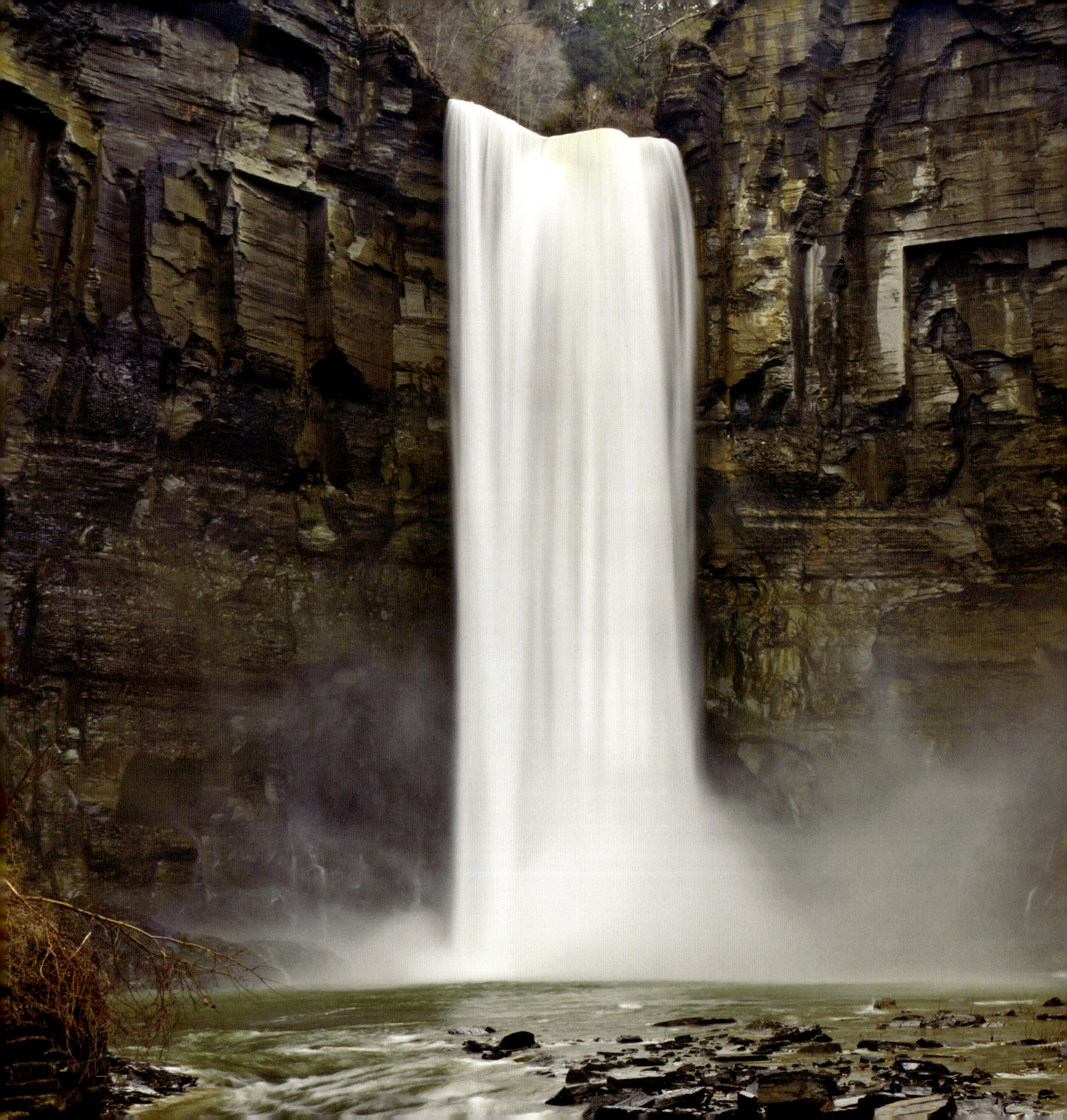

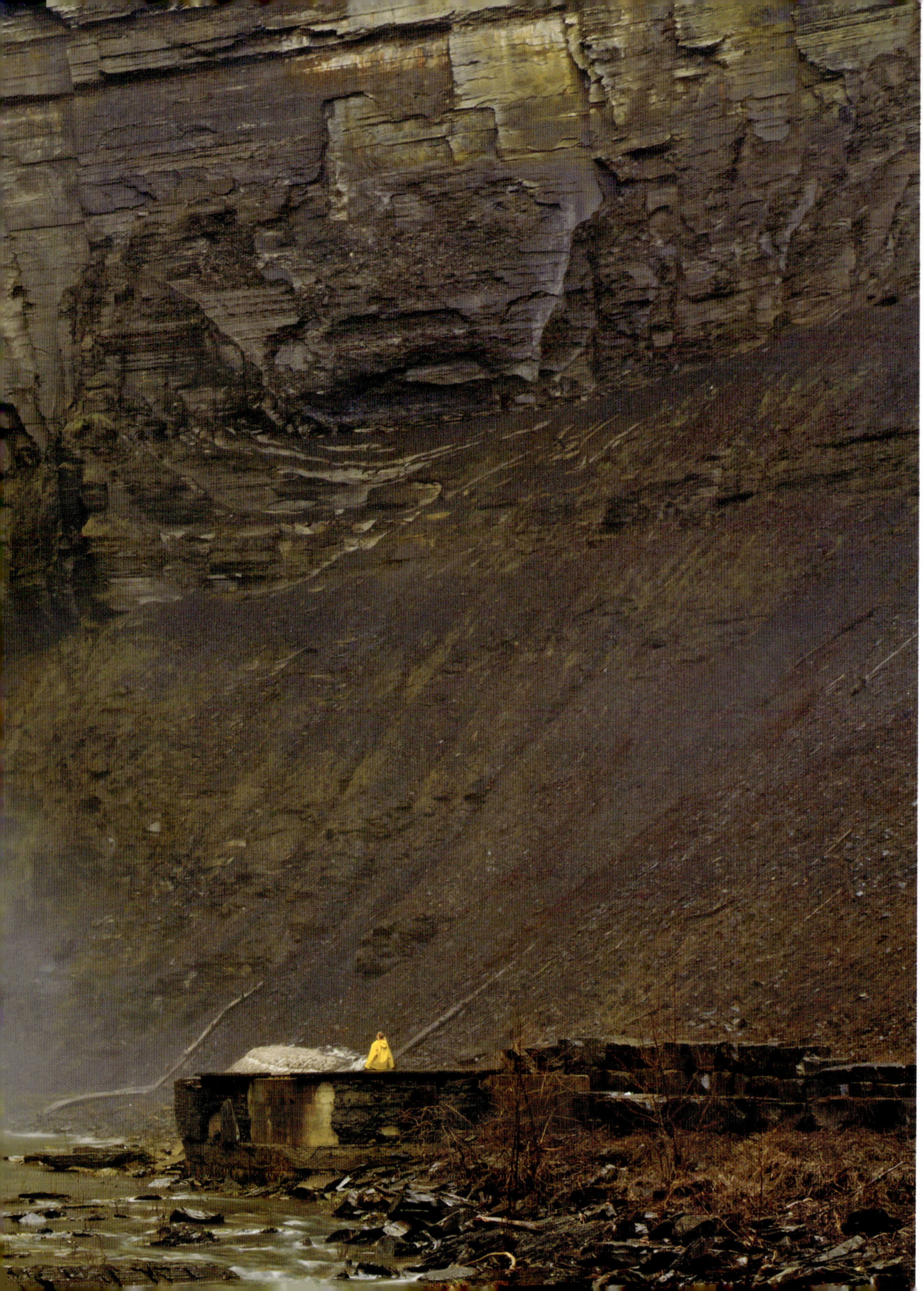

Taughannock State Park—one of the Finger Lake region's many state parks—features this 215-foot waterfall, one of the tallest in the eastern United States.

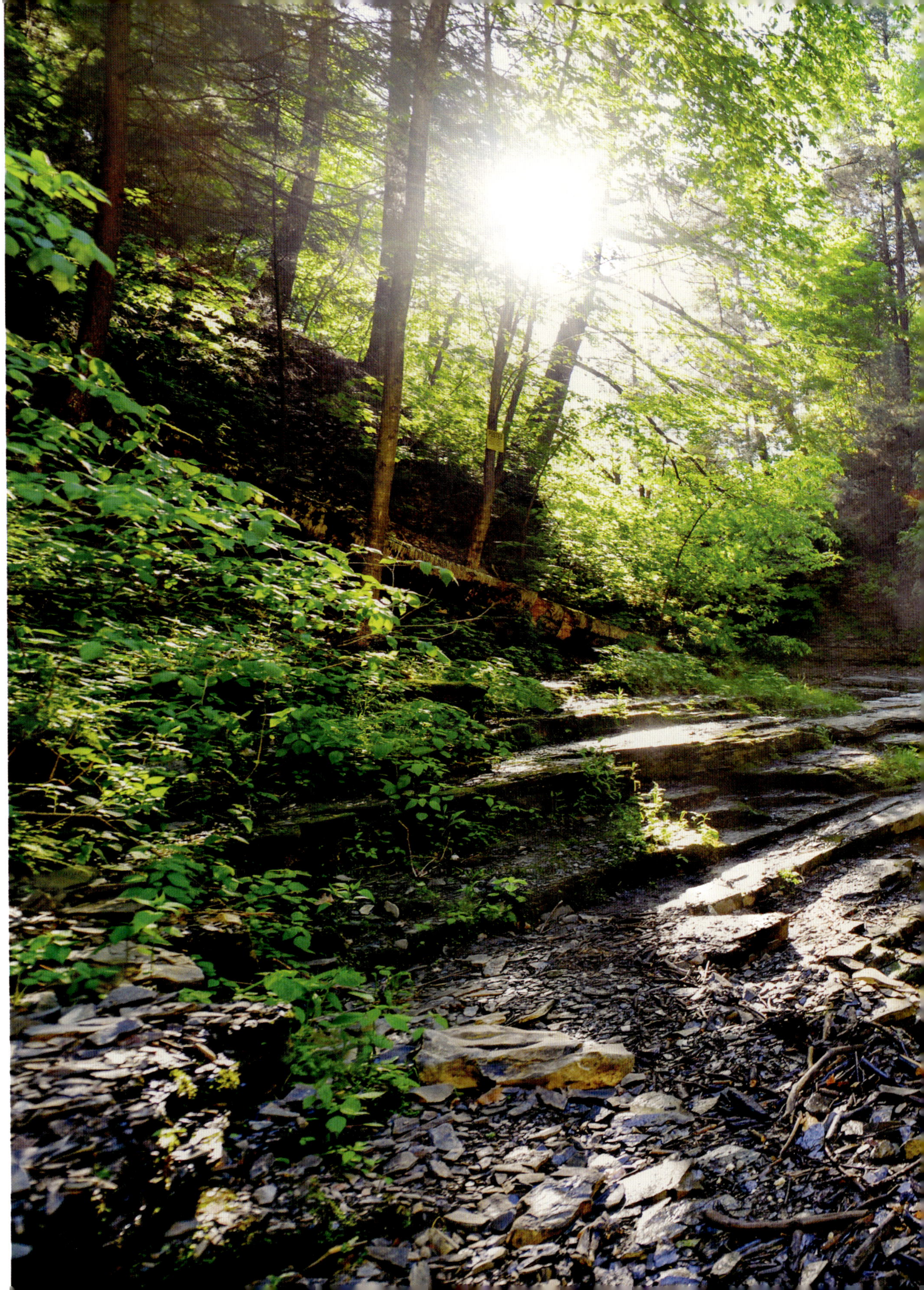

The natural rock amphitheater and wide creek of Havana Glen Park provides a unique opportunity for viewing wildlife; it is a home to over 100 species of birds, and migratory trout use the stream each season to travel from Seneca Lake to safely spawn.

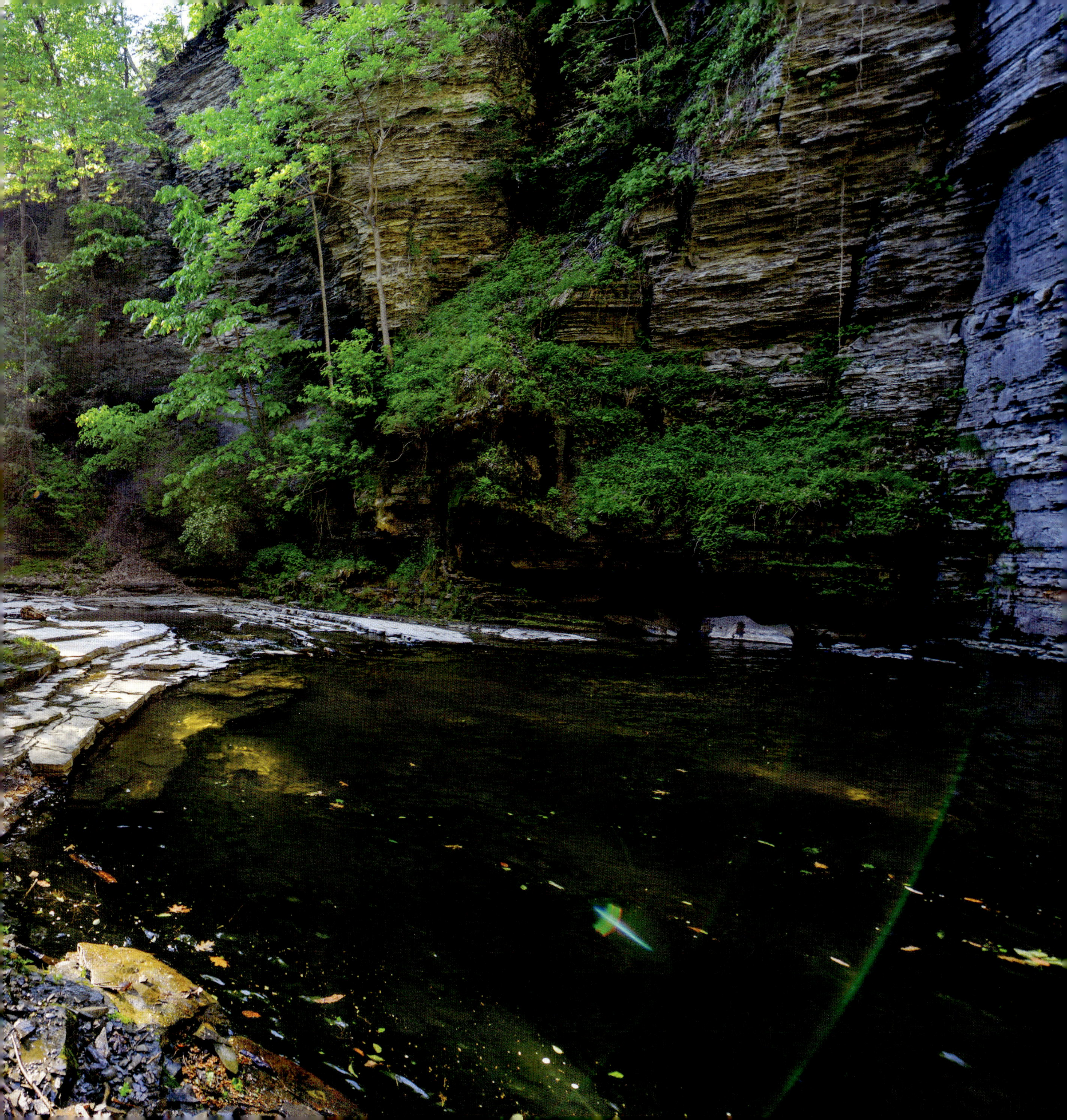

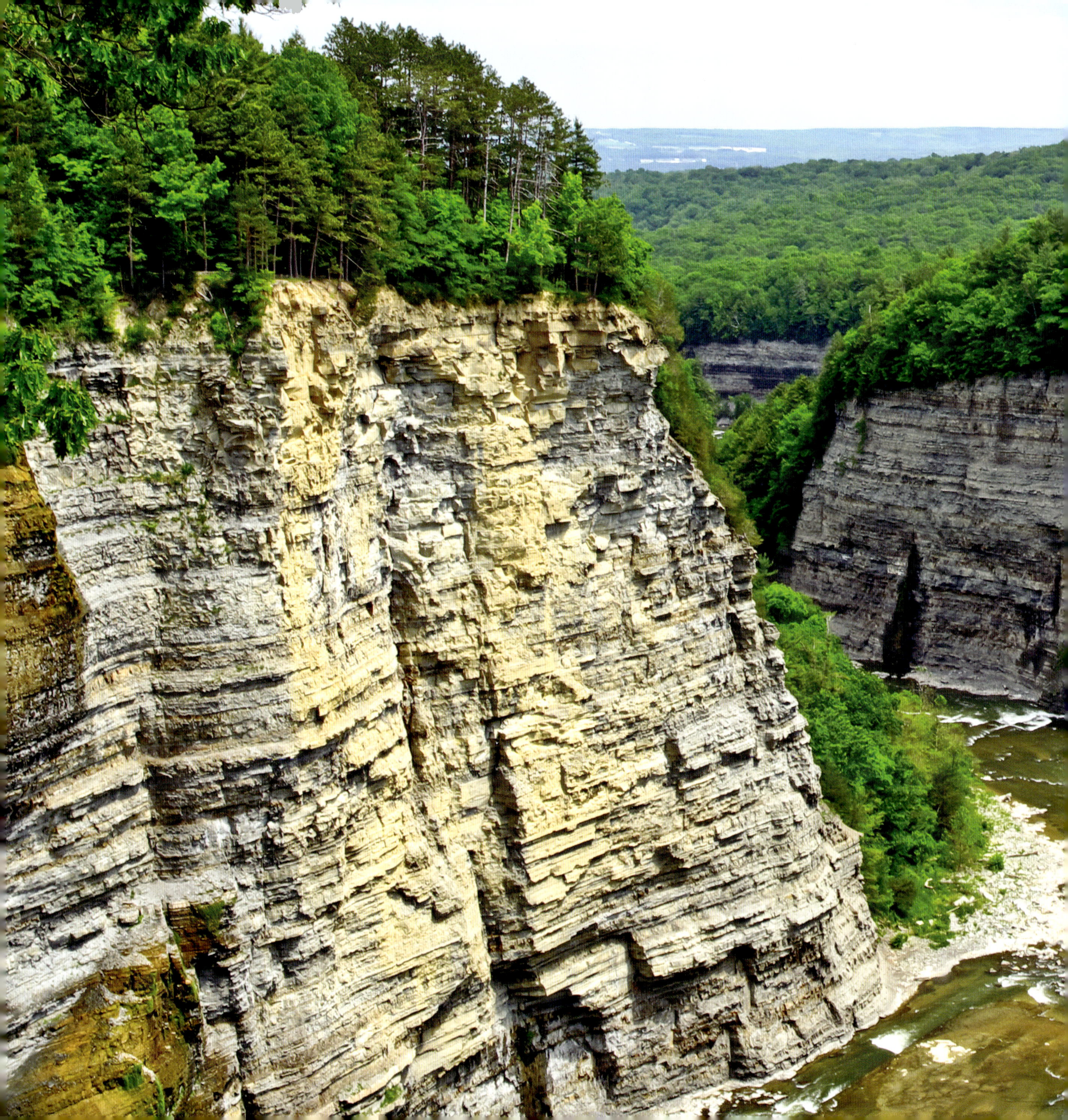

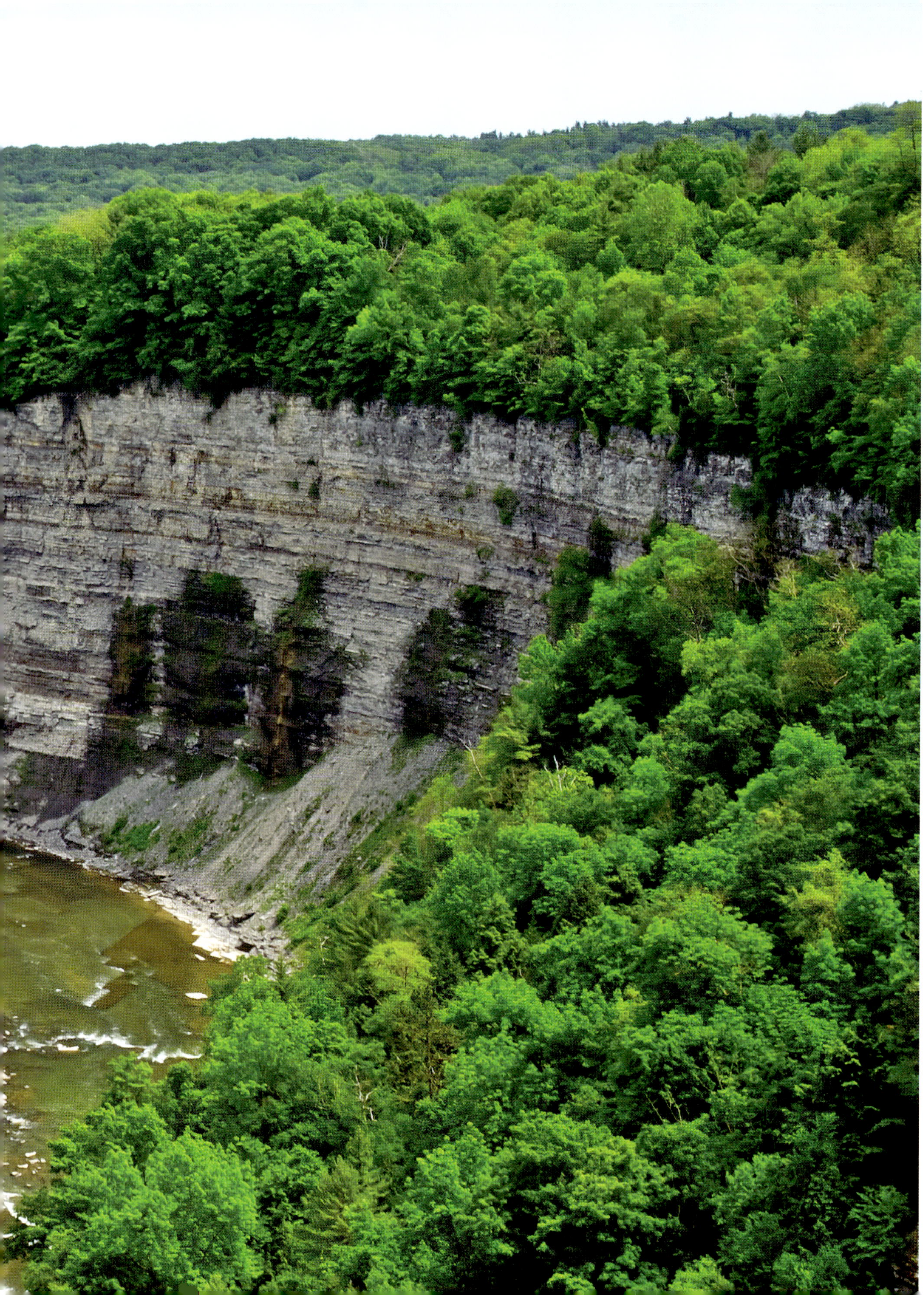

Rough-hewn shale, limestone, and sandstone gorges criss-cross Letchworth State Park along the Genesee River. Rock walls rise over 550 feet in places, earning the area the nickname of "Grand Canyon of the East."

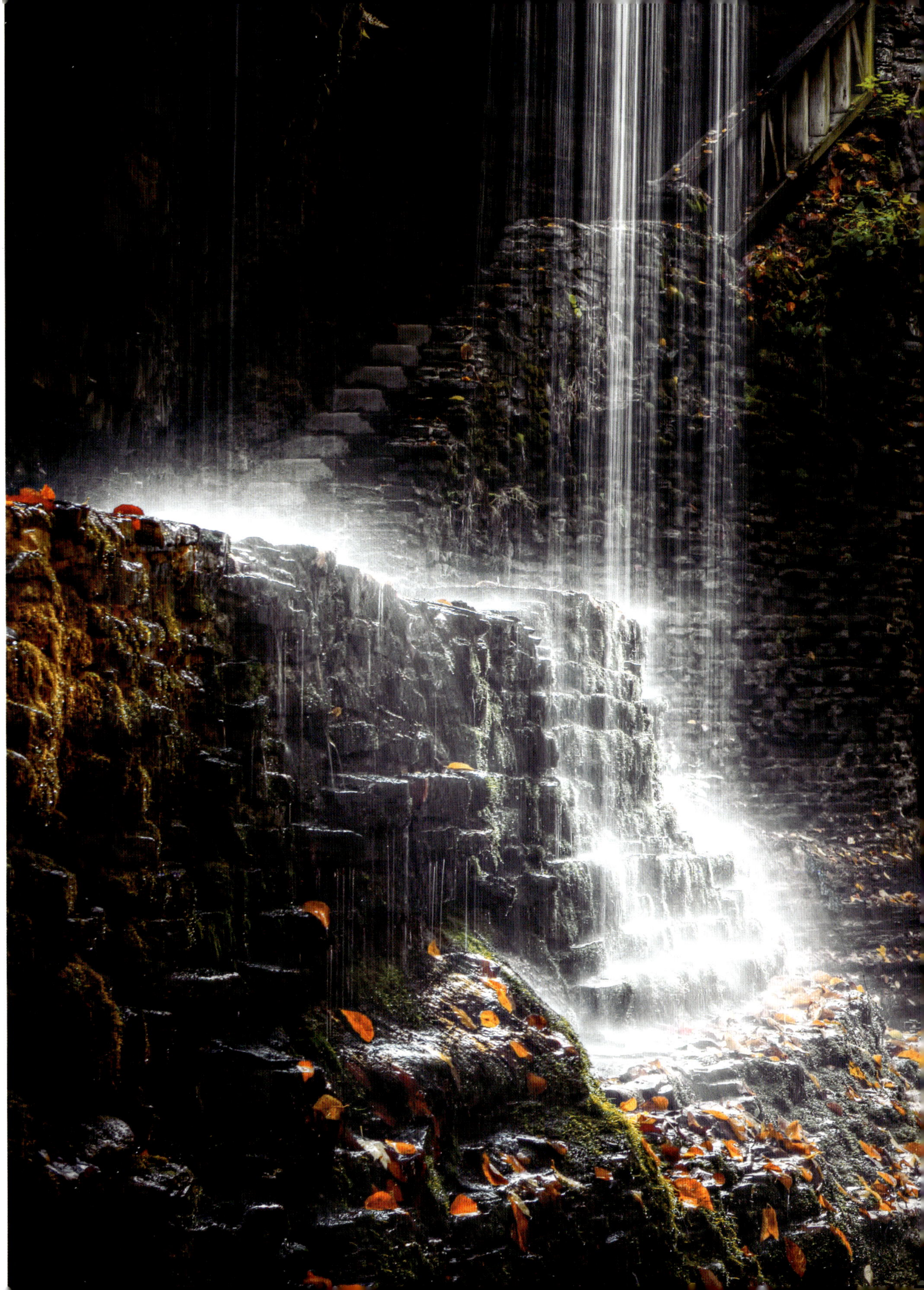

A stone pathway leads visitors behind the cascading Rainbow Falls. Here at the southern tip of Seneca Lake lies Watkins Glen State Park, a two-mile course home to 19 spellbinding waterfalls.

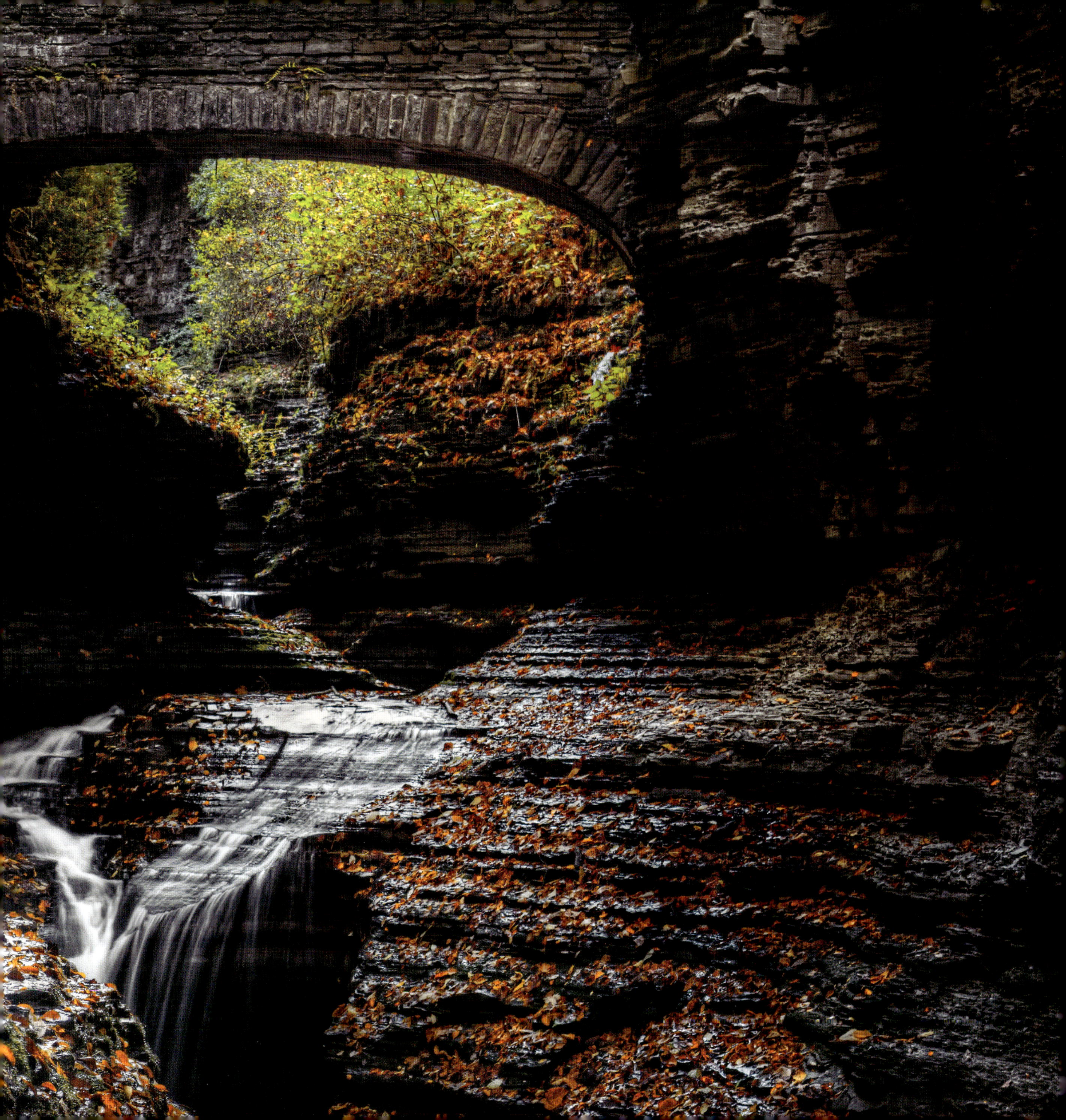

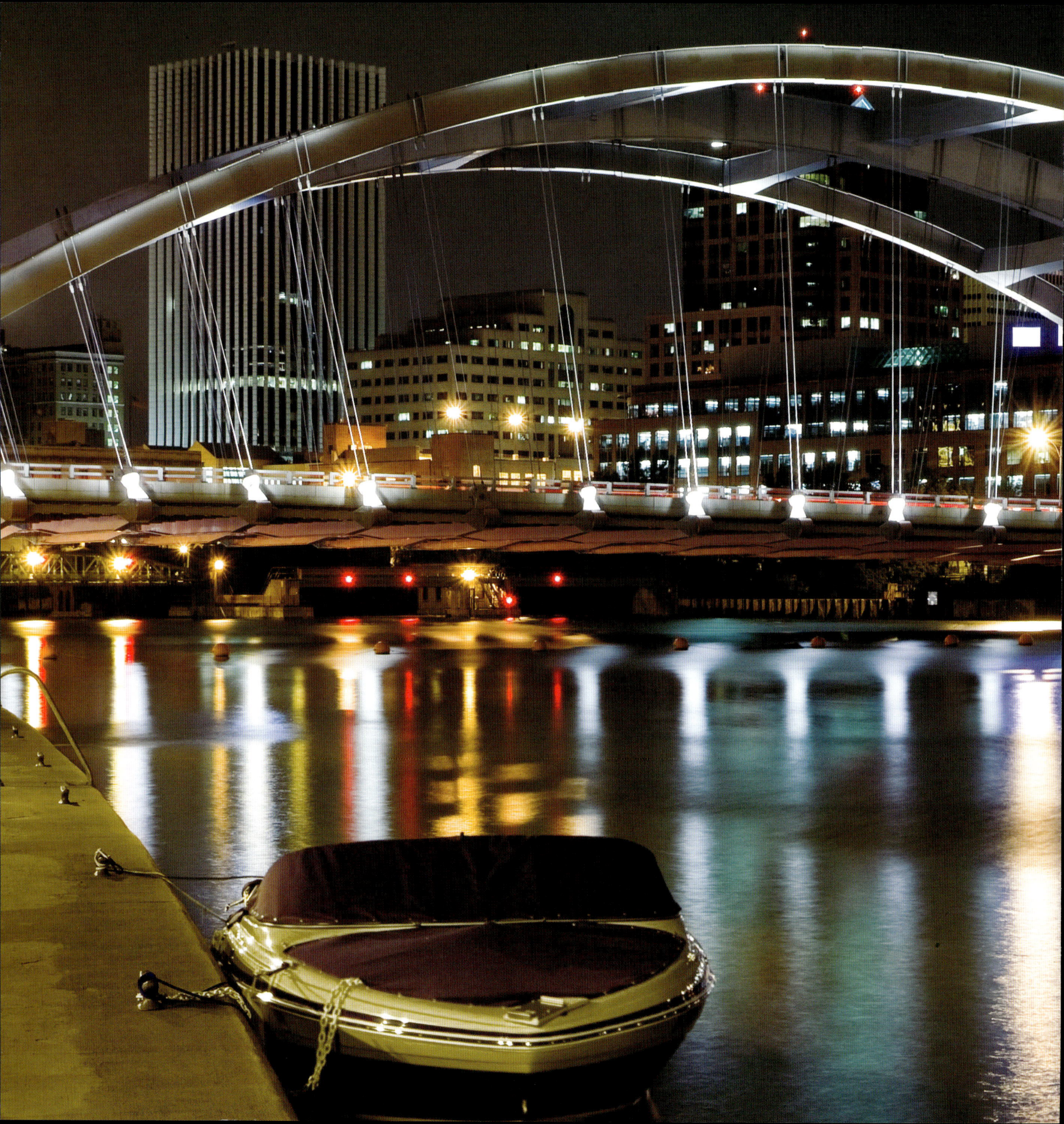

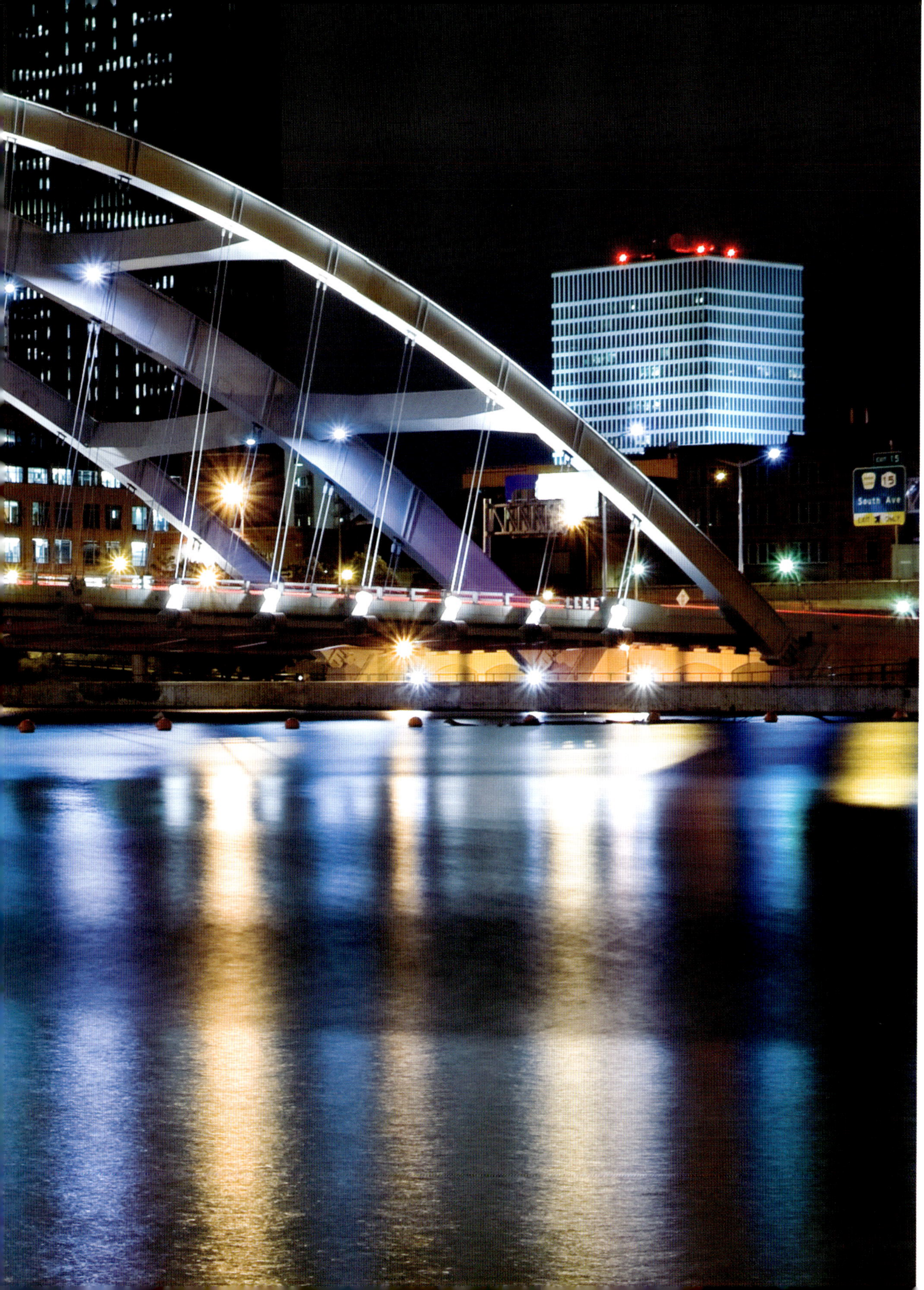

Birthplace to Kodak, Bausch & Lomb, and Xerox, with a prevalent imaging and optical science industry, the city of Rochester became known as the World's Image Center.

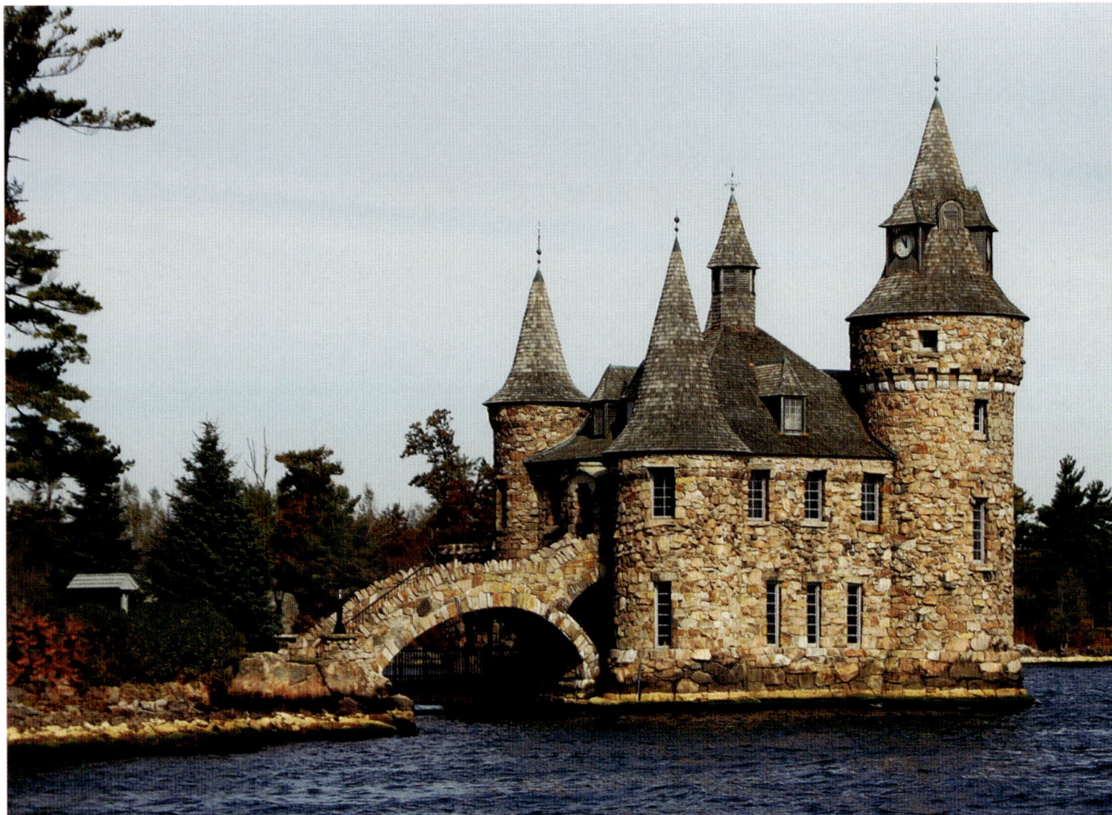

Open to public touring, the Power House of Boldt Castle sits upon Heart Island in the Thousand Islands region. These magnificent castles were built as island homes for yesteryear's wealthy landowners.

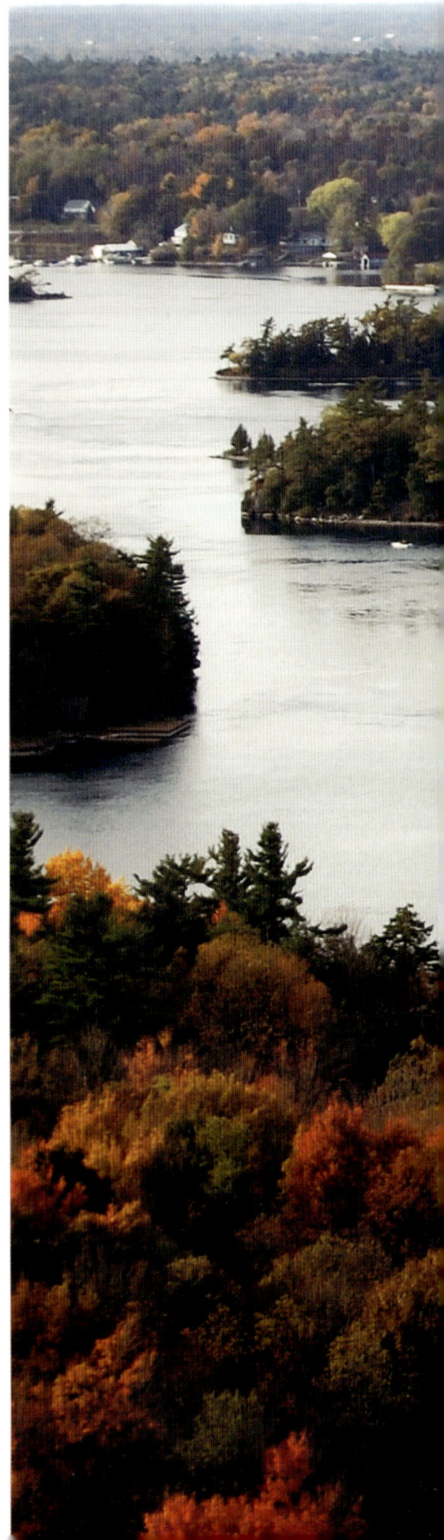

Like a fleet of tree-lined watercraft, the chain of 1,865 islands make up the Thousand Islands region in the St. Lawrence River

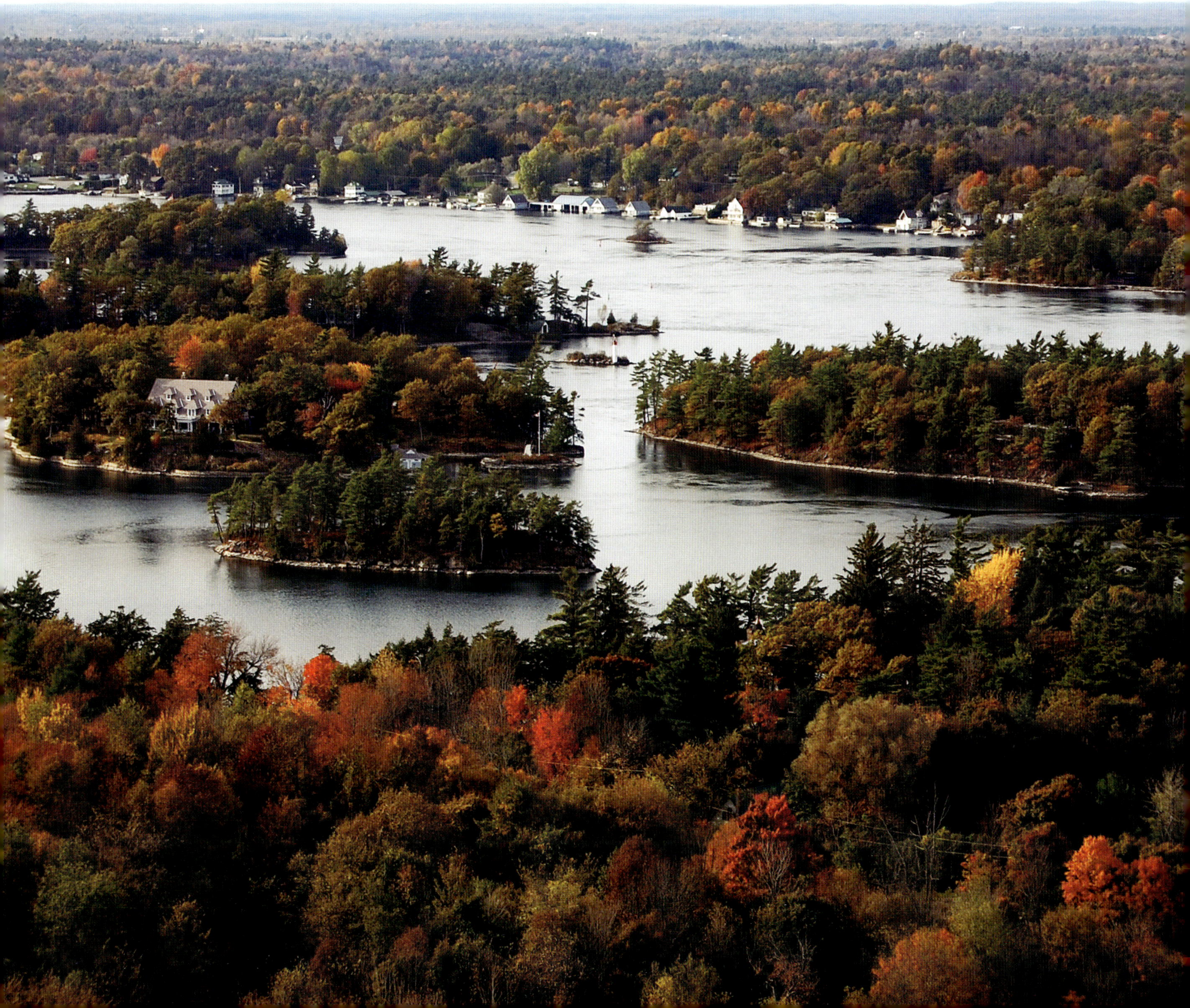

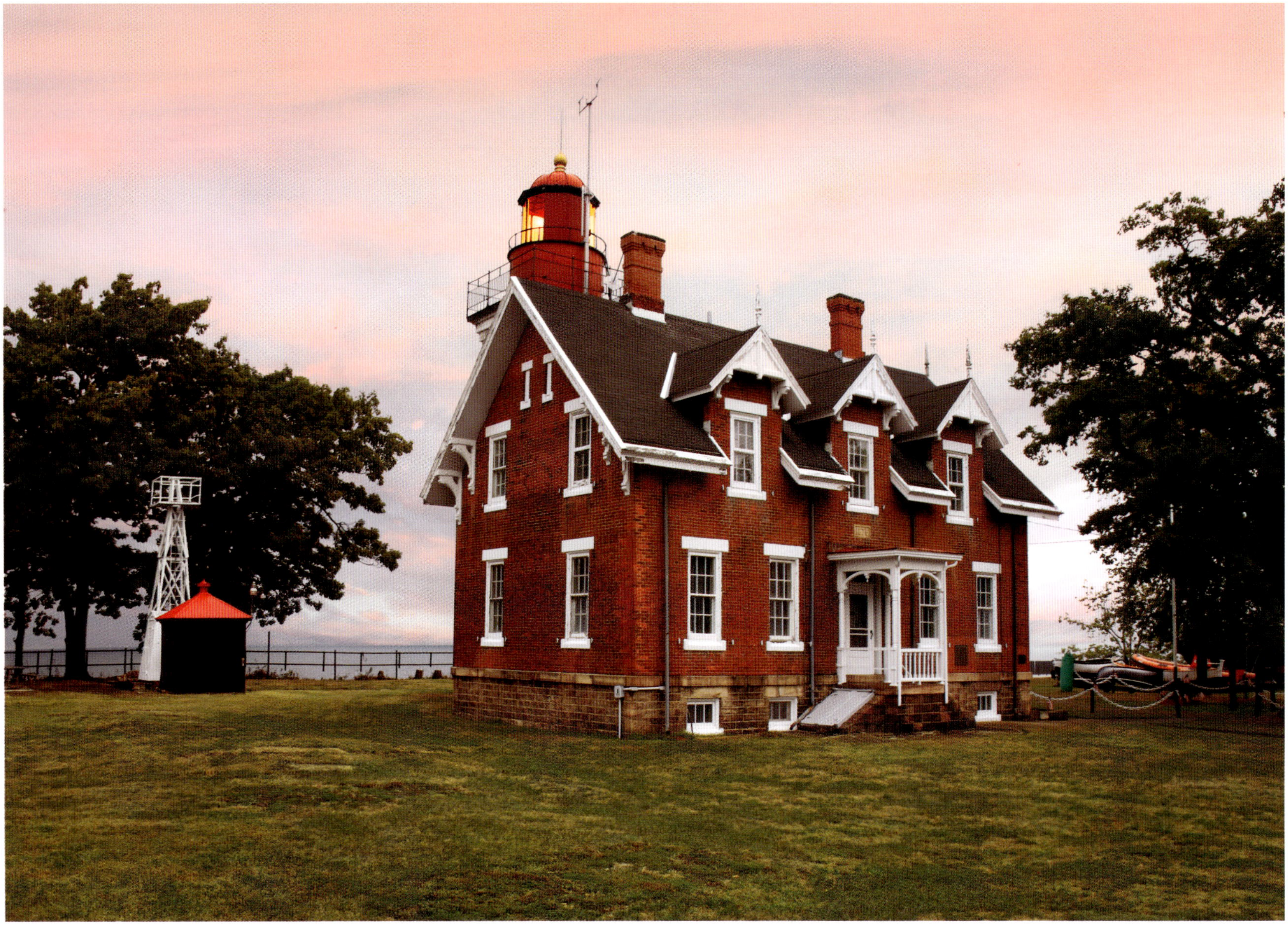

The historic Dunkirk Lighthouse overlooks Lake Erie at Point Gratiot. At approximately 210 miles long, and about 57 miles wide, Lake Erie is the 12th largest lake in the world.

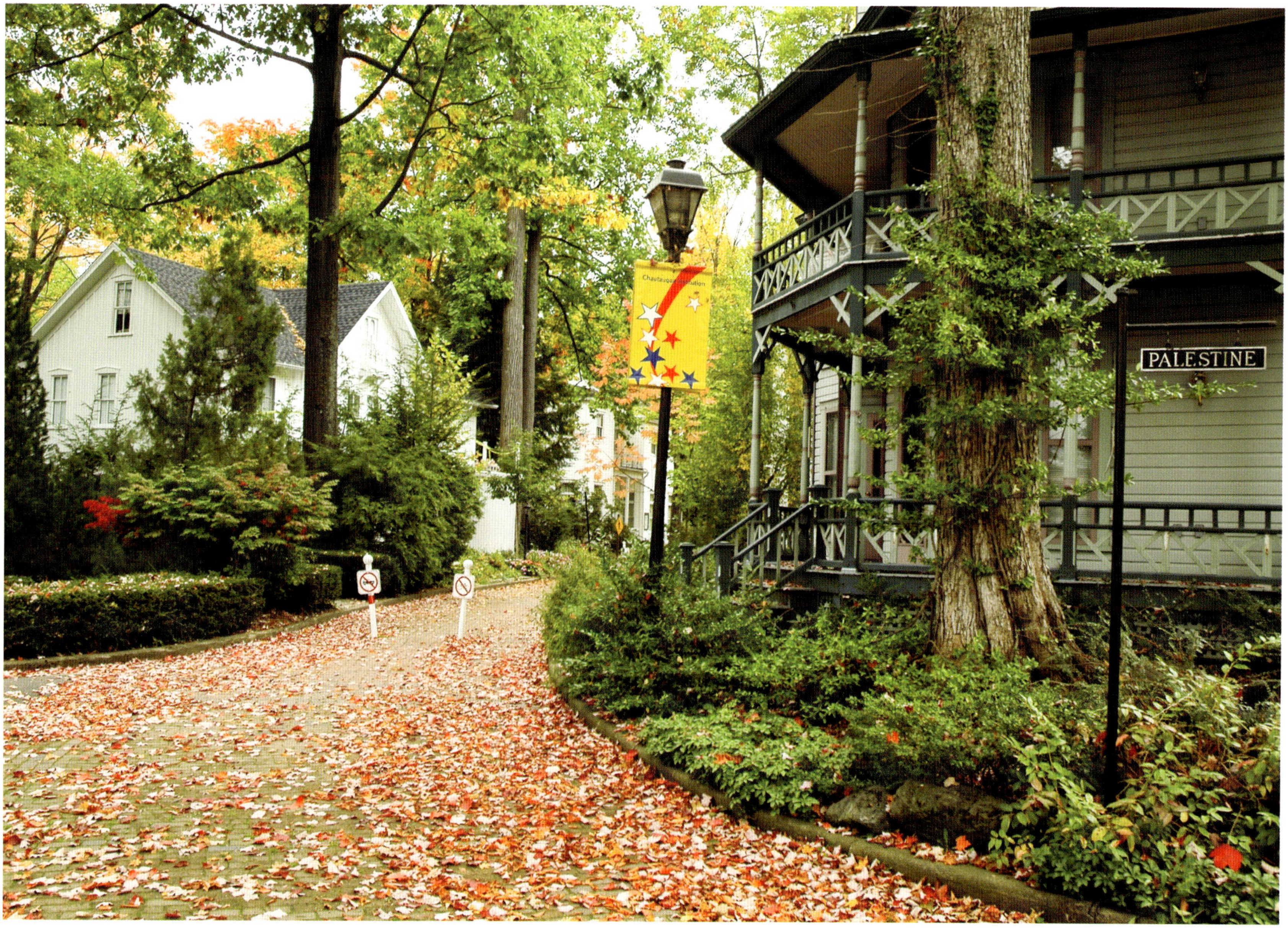

These Victorian buildings found near Jamestown are part of Chautauqua Institution, the original site of the late 1800s Chautauqua adult education movement, which was dedicated to bringing lecturers, music, and theater to the general public.

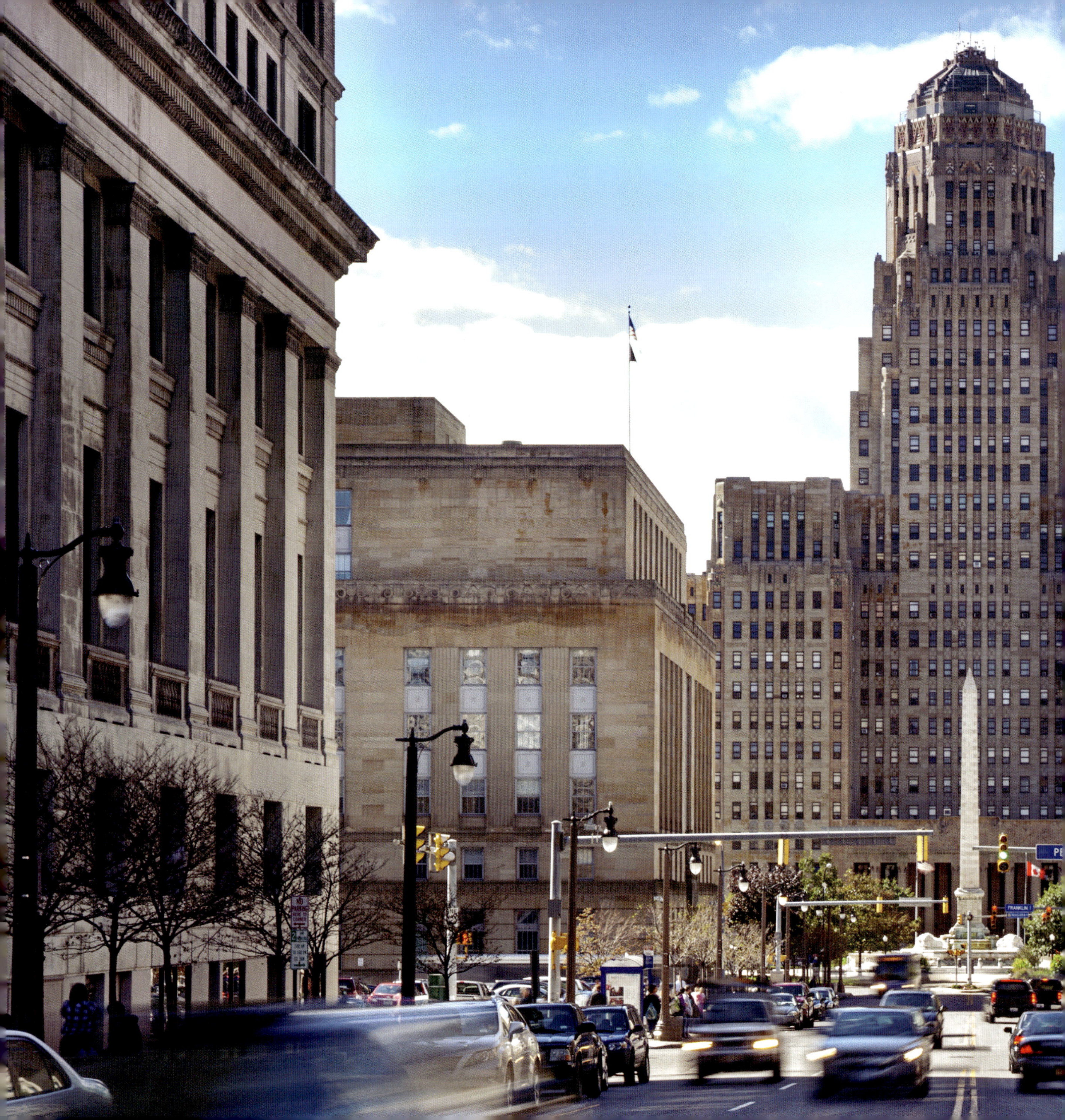
FRANKLIN

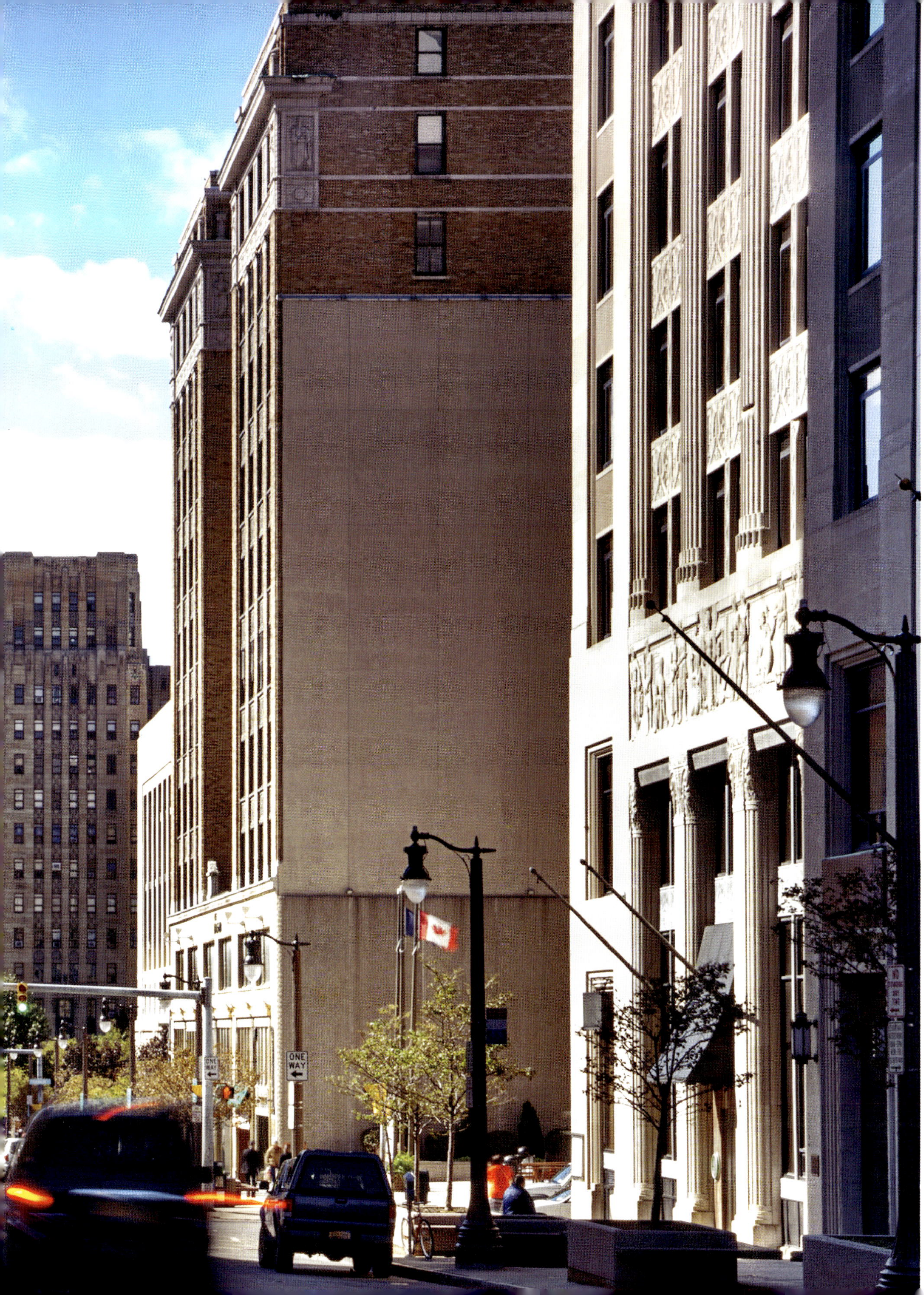

Situated on the Niagara River, Buffalo is New York's second largest city. The 32-story Art Deco city hall dominates the downtown business district.

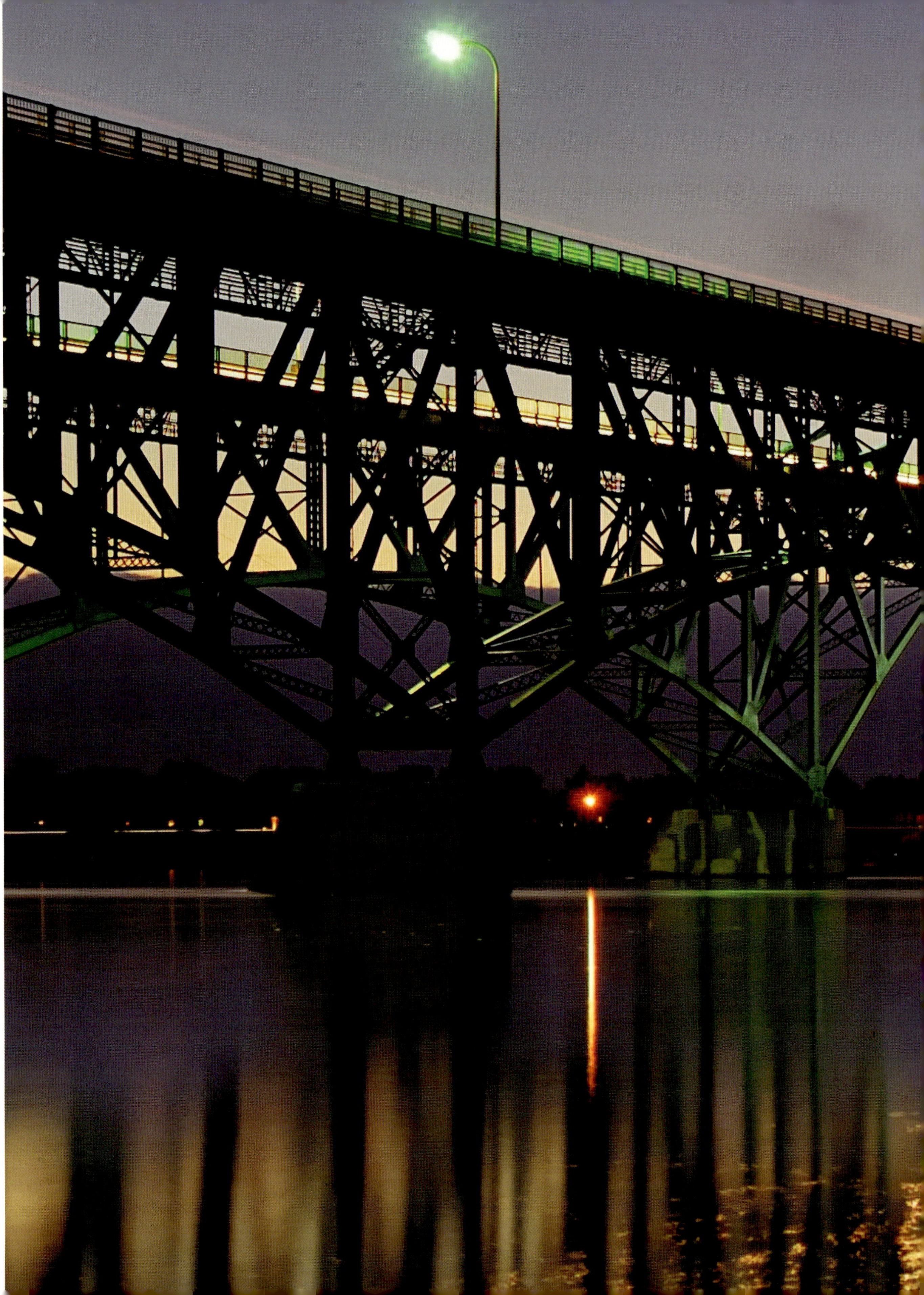

A shimmering reflection in the Niagara River captures South Grand Island Bridge, a pair of twin truss arch bridges. Though built decades apart, great care was taken in matching the style and architecture, and they appear nearly identical.

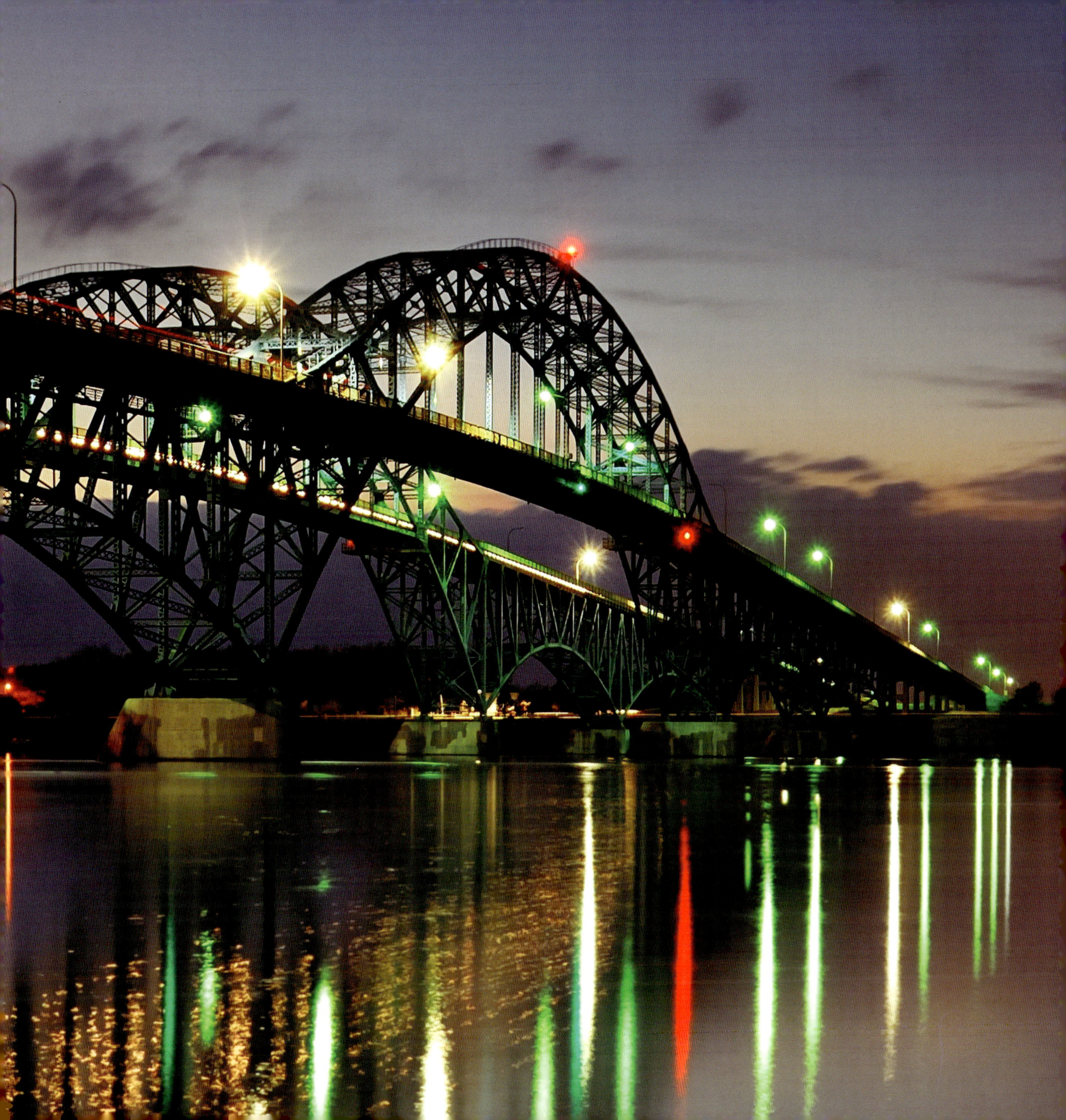

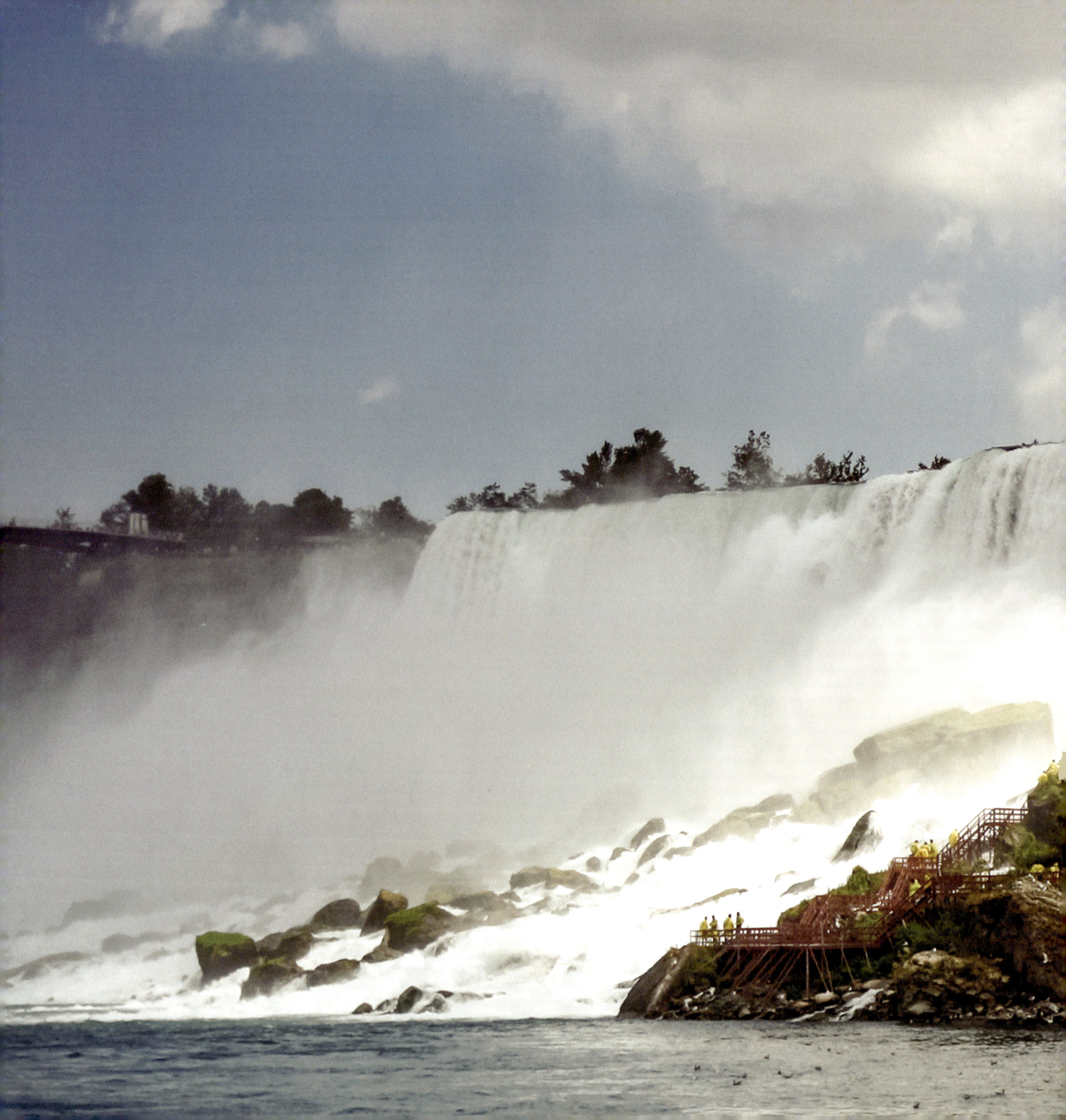

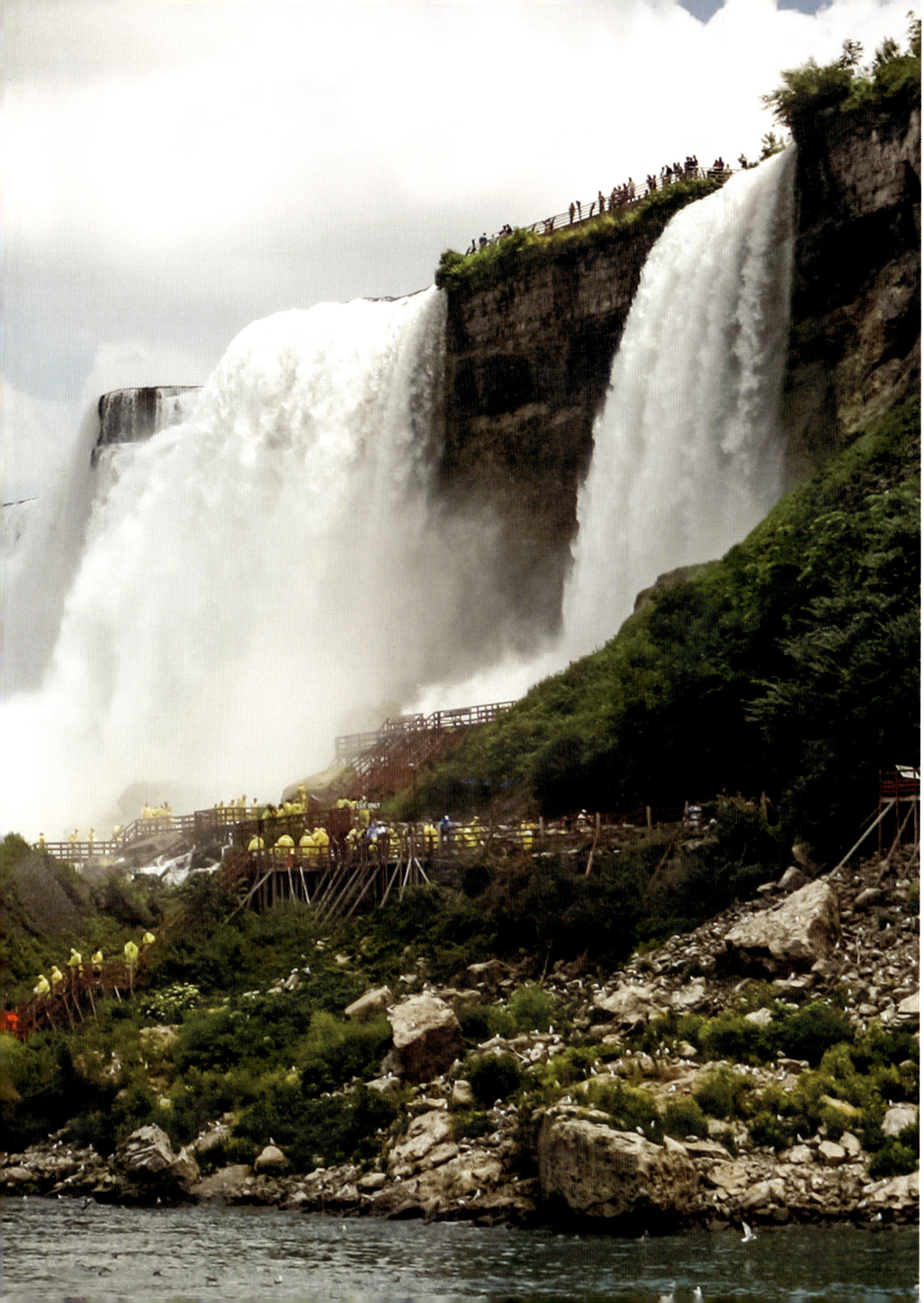

The journey ends at Niagara Falls, with its rushing water and rising mist, an icon of breathtaking natural wonder. Each minute, more than 40 million gallons of water plummet 180 feet over the Falls' ragged edge.

Photo Credits

Photri Microstock 6–7, 10, 11, 24, 25

Tom Till 8, 28, 66–67, 76

Walter Bibikow/Folio, Inc. 9, 15, 18–19

Patti McConville/Unicorn Stock Photos 12–13, 14, 23, 29, 38, 78

Bachmann/Unicorn Stock Photos 16–17

Bachmann/Photri Microstock 31

Paul Rezendes 20, 21, 22, 26–27, 32, 33, 42–43, 52–53, 54–55, 56–57, 83, 84–85, 86–87, 88–89

Andre Jenny/Unicorn Stock Photos 30, 39, 40, 46–47, 60, 61, 64, 65, 73

Gerry Lemmo 34, 59, 71, 79, 80–81, 82, 92

Michael Ventura/Folio, Inc. 35, 36, 37

Catherine Ursillo/Folio, Inc. 41

D & I MacDonald/Unicorn Stock Photo 44–45

D & I MacDonald/Photri Microstock 48

David Harp/Folio, Inc. 49

Mark Romesser/Unicorn Stock Photos 50–51, 58

Mark E. Gibson/Folio, Inc. 62, 63, 70

Unicorn Stock Photos 68–69

David Falconer/Folio, Inc. 72

Chuck Schmeiser/Unicorn Stock Photos 74–75

Colin D. Young 76-77

Jeff Greenberg/Photri Microstock 90

Jeff Greenberg/Folio, Inc. 91, 93, 94–95